"Where do we go from here?"

Ann Forster

To
Linda
with love and
best wishes.

Ann Forster.

Note for Librarians: A cataloguing record for this book is available from Library and Archives Canada at www.collectionscanada.ca/amicus/index-e.html
ISBN 1-4120-5520-2

Printed in Victoria, BC, Canada. Printed on paper with minimum 30% recycled fibre. Trafford's print shop runs on "green energy" from solar, wind and other environmentally-friendly power sources.

TRAFFORD

Offices in Canada, USA, Ireland and UK

This book was published *on-demand* in cooperation with Trafford Publishing. On-demand publishing is a unique process and service of making a book available for retail sale to the public taking advantage of on-demand manufacturing and Internet marketing. On-demand publishing includes promotions, retail sales, manufacturing, order fulfilment, accounting and collecting royalties on behalf of the author.

Book sales for North America and international:
Trafford Publishing, 6E–2333 Government St.,
Victoria, BC v8t 4p4 CANADA
phone 250 383 6864 (toll-free 1 888 232 4444)
fax 250 383 6804; email to orders@trafford.com
Book sales in Europe:
Trafford Publishing (uk) Limited, 9 Park End Street, 2nd Floor
Oxford, UK ox1 1hh UNITED KINGDOM
phone 44 (0)1865 722 113 (local rate 0845 230 9601)
facsimile 44 (0)1865 722 868; info.uk@trafford.com
Order online at:
trafford.com/05-0418

10 9 8 7 6 5 4

Dedications

To Jenny Jones, my friend and ongoing inspiration.

Martin, my best friend and husband – Thank you, I love you.

Sheelah Latham, for her friendship & incessant nagging!
Without her this book would not be in print.

"My gang" in the Spirit world, mum, dad, Freda, Louis, Irene,
Brian, to name but a few.

Love Ann

Contents

List of photos

These photos have been included for you to be able to put a face to the name as you read through the chapters.

Introduction

"When you're dead, you're dead!"

"Nobody ever comes back to tell us what it's like!"

These two statements are quotes, they were someone else's beliefs about death and Life after death or should I say lack of it. The first statement belonged to my father and the second to my mum. No wonder I thought I was going crazy when, at the age of 28, I naturally began the process of developing my mediumship and psychic ability. I say naturally because it simply started on its own, many people sit in spiritual development circles in order to trigger the spark or to harness and develop their already heightened intuition and spiritual awareness.

I'm sure you can imagine the internal conflict I was experiencing. My upbringing had me programmed to believe "when you're dead you're dead" but, I was now hearing voices both inside and at the side of my head, I was feeling and smelling unearthly smells and feelings, also I was seeing an array of spiritual and psychic spectacles. For many years I "lived" with my parent's beliefs or at least on the surface I did. As far back as I can remember, deep inside I had my doubts, I just knew there was something more, and I just hadn't discovered it.

When all the "weird and wonderful" things started to happen to me, I soon realised that these statements were wrong, and the conflict was soon over. I soon came to the conclusion that if I was having all these experiences and there wasn't any life after death, then it meant "I was out of my tree" and it was only a matter of time before "they would come and take me away!"

I have a number of reasons for writing this book, one being a message to people who, like I was in the past, are experiencing spiritual and psychic phenomena and may think they are losing their mind. The main reason has to be that I have worked as a professional medium since 1983. During that time I have been gathering knowledge, experiencing wonderful and emotional encounters with both Spirits and clients, which I now feel in a privileged position to share with anyone who wants to listen. This book also contains accounts of experiences gathered from family and friends not only clients, people have been very generous in allowing me to include their most private and precious memories of their encounters with the Spirit world.

1

So many people have had a spiritual experience or witnessed psychic activity, but they feel they dare not tell anyone about it for fear of being classed a "nutter" or at least being laughed at. I spent the early years of my life being one of these people; I know first hand how it feels. During my time as a medium I have met hundreds of people with a spiritual or psychic story to tell and on many occasions I have been told "what a relief to tell someone about it."

This book is aimed at all you people out there who feel they dare not tell anyone what they have seen or felt – you are not alone – feel privileged and among friends.

Very early on in my career I knew I would one day write this book, also I had no idea just how long it would take me to find the time or pluck up the courage to do it.

As I had gathered my information along the way I have asked permission for the person's experience to be included in this book. Most people were more than pleased and answered yes immediately. Some, though, were reluctant to be mentioned by name so I have kept them anonymous by using a fictitious name but that is all I have changed. It is still a very taboo subject for many people they could not bear to be judged or "branded"! There were, however, also many that were more than happy to "go public".

I feel a need to mention what it took to get this book into print. We will call it "The long haul!" I wrote the original manuscript by hand between 1996 & 1997, Martin, now my husband, edited it and in 1998 we started approaching publishers – many, many publishers! Following too many rejections to mention and one "near miss" in 1999 by a large publishing house used to publishing this type of book – I was rejected because I wouldn't offer them a celebrity client! I put the manuscript in a drawer, never forgot it, but hadn't the energy to do any more with it – until now. Thanks to the constant nagging of my friend Sheelah and the love and belief in me shown by Martin, I have found renewed faith, courage to publish the book myself!!!! I hope you find help, comfort or inspiration in it, but most of all, I hope you simply enjoy it.

Chapter One

Ann

My earthly life started on Saturday the 10th of October 1953 at 7.30 p.m. I was the second child of Henry and Annie, the first born being Marion, 7 years my senior; my brother Danny was born two years after me then a further two years produced my sister, Susan, the baby of the family.

Mum told me my dad showed great delight when he first set eyes on me. I had dark eyes and my skin had the appearance of a dark tan. Dad commented on this, he said, "She looks as though she's been on her holidays!" When he was alive he was a very visual person with a critical eye, I certainly appealed to him at that time, but I must point out this never gained me any special favours as I grew up. He was a great believer in "a fair day's work for a fair day's pay". Things had never come easily to him in life and he was determined to carry on in this mode. Not only with we four but also with my half sister Freda (passed to Spirit 1994) and half brothers Louis (passed to Spirit 2002) and Harry. Their mother Jane had died when she was only 34, Annie was my father's second wife.

My mum Annie was 11 years my Dad's junior, I felt she was a really good mum, very caring and dedicated to her children. She was over protective, the results of which materialised in later years; I can speak only for myself here. I realised I suffered from lack of ambition and limited confidence. When we were growing up as a family together we felt safe and protected. Short sighted at the time, but we must have felt we had everything we needed around us, there was no desire to search for more either internally or externally and mum must have felt the same, however life changes and then there is the realisation that one is not equipped!

Looking back on my upbringing I can describe the earlier years as "bordering on Victorian". Priorities were being well mannered, respecting my elders and discretion and dignity at all costs. I clearly remember not long before my father passed to Spirit, having to fight back my tears at my aunt's funeral just in case he saw me, he would have considered this as "letting the side down". Regardless of this rather "stiff" upbringing I have always been glad that I was born to these people, there are lots of things I would like to have changed about my childhood but I wouldn't like to have changed my parents.

Most households had and still have taboo or forbidden topics of conversation, ours was no exception, being ghosts and sex. On reaching my twenties and having left home after getting married at 22,

I had time to reflect, I came to the conclusion that my father did not like to talk about things, which embarrassed or frightened him. It wasn't to long before I had to dismiss this theory, at least with regard to sex, as I reminded myself that he had produced seven living children! Seriously though, like so many people, it is the fear of the unknown or the unexplained that make people announce statements like "all that rubbish". When they are faced with the vast subject of the paranormal, the shutters come down and they don't want to think about it, let alone talk about it or listen to more.

As far back as I can remember, I have been afraid of the dark. It's only now that I'm older and have gained knowledge, that I am able to understand why I felt afraid, after all I couldn't see anything to make me feel that way. Children are extremely sensitive and aware. I was no exception, through the dark I could feel or sense something very strongly even though I could not see anything to alarm me, this developed into fear. When I cried or objected to being put into the dark I would be told "don't be silly there's nothing there". I wonder how many of us have experienced similar feelings and made some kind of objection, having also been told this! How many people reading this book have said these words to their own children? Even from a very early age this creates an amazing amount of conflict in our minds, it certainly did in mine.

I believe that there are Spirits around us constantly; they live in a world (the Spirit World), which exists in another dimension or vibration. Therefore they cannot be seen unless they choose to show themselves to us. My interpretation of the thing that separates our two worlds is a curtain or fine gauze; sometimes the Spirits transcend this gauze, giving us a variety of spiritual experiences, many of which I have been privileged to witness.

I want to say this book has been written on belief, my belief and the belief of the many people who have contributed to it. My wish is that you read it and then make up your own mind; it may cause you to redress your own belief system.

Going back to the taboo subjects in our household of Spirits and ghosts, you may be saying to yourself, "This subject isn't discussed in every home" that's true, however, there was a problem; our house was haunted. From as far back as I can remember there had been "happenings" I speak for us all, except my dad, we did experience spiritual and psychic events, I always had my suspicions that he did also, but his fear and sense of pride forbade him to acknowledge the experience. You can imagine how this made life quite difficult for the rest of the family.

We did tell mum about the "goings on", the sound of footsteps that followed us upstairs, the door being gently pushed open as we were sitting on the loo, the vision of the lady walking across the landing that my brother witnessed on various occasions over a number of years, and many many more experiences. Firmly implanted in my mind is the voice of my mother saying, "don't let your dad hear you".

It was mum who used to say; "nobody ever comes back to tell us what it's like". She did openly admit to us but only when we were older, that she did really believe in Spirits. She couldn't have said too much because my dad would have disapproved. I felt sad that she had had to keep her beliefs to herself (you will discover the twist in the tale later in the book). I also thought "what a relief" there was someone on our side, the experiences we were all having were real, which also meant we weren't going mental after all! To me this felt like a turning point, it also felt like gaining a sense of freedom both of speech and to believe. Thanks mum for that and for sharing with me the story of your visits on Friday evenings to a local farmhouse, with a group of friends when you were a young woman, to attend "table-rapping sessions". These accounts used to make me get Goosebumps all over but I did love them!

The process of writing this book has demanded that I spend lot of time reflecting on my life, also searching through my mental archives for personal and client experiences, which have been stored away in a mental filing cabinet. It has also caused me to start asking questions like "why me?" "Why did I become a medium?" I'm nobody special - I thought, far from it, just an ordinary "lass from Lancashire" with an average but good quality general education, leaving school with two GCE and two CSE. I worked for a short time after leaving school for a local accountant, which didn't work out so I went working in various shops that covered a period of 10 years. I know that working with the general public was a wonderful training ground which taught me a lot about handling people and would come in very useful at a later date, when I started doing my spiritual work.

I have been economical with facts and details about myself at this stage, the reason for this is simply that the book isn't about me, it's about my work and mainly about other people. Good relationships and friendships are those that start slowly and develop with time, I hope you get to know me through my writing as you read the book. Someone gave me some advice a few years ago when we discussed the possibility of my writing this book. He said "write it in your own words", that's what I have done, by being myself you will get to know me, you will soon find out I'm a storyteller not a writer.

From left: Marion (holding Susan), Harry, Cynthia (sister in law), Danny Jarvis, Louis and Irene, Dad (Danny in front), Bill (brother in law), Mum, Freda. The only time the family were photographed together!

Chapter Two

Mediumship

$1$982 was a very significant year for me, so many things were going wrong, and my life felt like a catalogue of disasters. As the year changed from 1981 to 1982 I felt as though I was walking on very uneven ground, I entered the year feeling unhappy and uncertain about the future of my marriage. My friendships seemed to be dissolving before me with no real reasons why. The small pottery party plan business I was running, which had got off to a flying start the previous year enabling me to leave the clothes shop that I had worked in for years, but had grown to hate, this just ran dry.

I was terribly upset when my Party Plan business failed because pots and glassware were my passion. I got great joy out of selling them and I felt I did my job very well, so this disappointment was another negative emotion to go on the pile with all the rest. As you can imagine I was beginning to feel like one of life's failures. I had always tried to be a very positive person, too positive for my own good, a friend once told me "you've got a long way to fall down when things go wrong" nevertheless, "positive Annie" that's me.

I couldn't fathom out why everything was going wrong for me; I asked all the usual questions "am I a bad person? Does someone out there hate me?" Of course I didn't get any answers from anywhere to my questions. As I moved further into the year I could soon see that, I wasn't a failure, I wasn't a bad person, all this was meant to happen, a clearing away of the old in order to make way for the new.

The business was the first area to collapse along with some friendships, next was my marriage. In the June of 1982 I discovered that my husband was "gay", for many months I had suspected him of seeing someone else - another woman - or so I thought. In the May I visited a medium in Manchester called Dee Campion, she told me my husband was not interested in other women and she left it to me to draw my own conclusions! This I did and by June the truth was out, "what a relief" I thought, nobody could blame me for this, it was nature, nothing that I could have prevented. Once the dust had settled, the reality hit me; I was 28, feeling very lost and very much a failure in life in a general sense. There seemed nothing to look forward to, even though I stayed with my husband until the following March of 1983, the marriage was over, relationship wise I felt very lonely and could see that situation reaching out into the future. I was only skilled at selling. I had done shop work for 10 years and had watched my father revolve his life around his shop. He was a master butcher, even though he owned his own shop in the later years of his butchering career, he spent long, long hours at work. I didn't want this for myself in the future; yet at that time I felt doomed to it - what else could I do?

July 1982 was probably the weirdest month in my life. Life was very easy at that time yet very mundane. My daily life was uneventful, apart from dealing with feelings relating to the discovery of my husband's homosexuality. There was very little stress so, I just couldn't understand why I was feeling so tired and drained, I couldn't put my mind to anything, not only was there a lack of concentration but I couldn't think straight.

After a few weeks of not sleeping, I began to feel totally exhausted "brain dead" is how I prefer to describe this state. I would burst into tears at the drop of a hat. Many were the days that I would get up, make a drink and find I didn't have the energy to get dressed. Often I was still in my dressing gown at lunchtime. I would often "find myself" just sitting, staring into thin air. I say, "find myself" because, I would suddenly look around the room and I would need a period of adjustment. I was filled with a sense that I had been somewhere else, yet I couldn't say where; I had no memory of what had happened within my head during these last minutes. I referred to it as a visit to "no man's land".

I did find out years later, that this is not unusual or unique to me, a number of people have told me about "lost time" for some it has been minutes, for others, days.

At first it happened often. I did put it down to hormones or the stress created by my marital situation. After a couple more weeks of feeling ill and useless, things started to change; I started to sense Spirit people around me. It was not the first time in my life that I had experienced such situations, however, this was different. It was considerably stranger, very unnerving at times. At the start I used to sense their presence next they started to touch me. Sometimes the experience was overwhelming, one thing they did was give me the sensation of a pin being stabbed into me, at first I would jump and yelp, they did carry on until I found the sense to tell them to stop. By doing this, at least it was an acknowledgement from me that I knew; "they" were there. It was our earliest form of conscious communication, if any of us asks someone to stop doing something, the logic is, that they must be there in the first place.

Stage two was gentler, in many ways more exciting, the feeling of a hand placed softly on my shoulder. I have to admit that this did take a lot of getting used to. I have to be truthful and say that at first I really didn't like it, nonetheless they carried on with their touching and stroking, sometimes a kiss on the cheek or head. This is the time that I realised what was happening to me - I panicked, I had read about other people becoming mediums, everyone's story is quite unique a different process of realisation, a different time of their lives, everyone's story very different from the next person's. Oh questions, questions! "What do I do now?", "who do I tell?" Moreover, the classic question "why me?" There was one thing I knew for sure, I didn't want to be like this!

My only experiences of "dabbling" with the Spirit world in the past had been a séance and two visits to mediums for spiritual readings. The séance was in the medical room when I was at secondary school (I'm still convinced to this day that, this was instrumental in opening my mind to spiritual communications.). These had left me feeling very unnerved, without a doubt in my mind that I was being watched, and I didn't really like it.

Referring back to the question "why me?" exactly, why me? I would never have considered myself suitable material to become a medium, too timid, too nervous. I also wondered why had the two mediums I had visited for readings never told me about all this, they could have warned me I thought. At a later date, I was reading through the notes I had taken down during my readings and discovered in fact the lady, Dee Campion had done so. It was very cleverly "wrapped up" I suppose this was done in order that I would not panic, and that was the right thing to do, I'm sure I would have gone "bananas". This lady told me that I had a natural gift that I would use in a teaching situation, the passing on of knowledge to others. It really didn't make much sense to me at the time but most readings very rarely do.

It didn't take me long to get used to being "touched". When it didn't happen for a while, a few days or a week, I started to wonder what was wrong, had they deserted me? Or did they not need me anymore? It was never very long before the communication resumed; seems silly to say this now but it was a relief.

Things in general seemed to settle down, not just spiritually but generally in my life. I had really accepted the fact that even though my marriage was over and Terry and I were living as friends, that situation couldn't go on indefinitely, however sharing a house was fine for that time. A little time passed and then the next stage of development began - the clairvoyance. One Monday morning I was vacuuming my bedroom when suddenly I was stopped in my tracks, a clear and colourful picture flashed up in my mind, it was as vivid as a page from a magazine, and the picture was of my cousin Barbara. I hadn't seen her for quite some time. I remember being stopped in my tracks and saying out loud, "Oh Barbara" even though I have always had a very vivid imagination, I can honestly say I had never experienced anything like this before. Once I had got over the shock I continued with my chore.

At lunchtime of that day there was a knock on my front door; it won't be difficult to guess who it was. Yes, Barbara. I greeted her with "I knew you were coming!" In she came and we entered into a lengthy discussion about this "picture". She was fascinated; we discovered we both shared a strong interest in these mystic matters. Barbara was extremely supportive towards me at this early stage of my acceptance and development. This was a very small occurrence when compared to the spiritual experiences that would follow over the years; however, from small acorns great oak trees grow!

Many people have clairvoyant flashes, they are a "one-off" or occasional, mine just kept on happening, and they made a lot of sense very quickly. Some of the early experiences seem very petty now but I will tell you, as this may happen to you, if you take notice of these experiences; who knows where it will lead?

I was preparing tea one day; I picked up a beautiful looking potato, as I picked up the knife to start preparing it I saw a "flash" of a black hole inside. I proceeded to slice it in two and there was the black crater, I dropped the knife in shock. Then there were incidents such as listening to the radio and "knowing" which song would follow the one that was already playing. I would guess that, from time to time everybody has these experiences, it is when they start to occur day in and day out that it causes one to question "what is going on?"

I have a vivid memory of my first clairaudient experience (hearing Spirit); I was fast asleep but woke abruptly. I felt as though I had been "switched on" like someone had flicked on a light switch, I felt wide-awake; I had my bearings instantly (I was alone that night so I knew I could not have been disturbed by a human being). This voice was a female Spirit, it was calm and clear, she spoke at the side of my left ear, and the voice was not inside my head. I questioned later – "was this the voice of a living person?" The answer had to be no. There was no one in the house, only me.

She told me that everything was going to be all right, which I feel referred to my personal situation. This was a very strange but extremely magical experience. I have become so used to hearing voices that it is second nature now, but looking back on this experience has made me realise just how special this and any kind of spiritual communication is.

The next morning I knew the time had come to seek help. I contacted a medium that at that time lived in the Manchester area, his name was Stephen Kirk, and he had come highly recommended to me. He was a super medium and a wonderfully warm human being. I do owe so much to him for being my mentor and guide in those early days of mediumship development. Over twenty years later I still talk about Stephen, I quote him, chapter and verse. He told me about both the joys and the struggles of being a medium; these have proved themselves to be true. One statement is etched on my mind, he said "this is how it is, there's not a bloody thing you can do about it, your feet are on the road, now get walking", so I did!

Chapter Three.

"How do you know?"

If I had a pound for every time someone has asked me the question "how do you know these things?" during the years that I have worked as a professional medium, then I would have quite a nice little "nest egg" by now.

This question was seconded by "what does it feel like?" It is very difficult to begin answering these questions. Only a medium or psychic would fully comprehend what I say, nevertheless I shall attempt to answer these questions yet again for you. In the past I always felt that there was something missing from my explanation, today I shall try to put that right.

Before I start breaking this down and maybe getting technical, I would like to say that, when the sixth sense which I believe we all have, starts to operate it is such a weird yet wonderful experience, it's virtually impossible to put into words. A few years ago I was on a Neuro Linguistic Programming advanced communication course in Manchester, I allowed a colleague from the course to use me as the subject of her modelling project. Using the skills that we were taught on the course she was able to break down and analyse the process of spiritual communication to a very fine level. I found this very intrusive, almost disrespectful to the Spirits. The work session continued for two hours (what I found interesting was, we had taped the session and when it was over, nothing had been recorded, regardless of the fact that the tape was running). When it was over the lady left and I was left with a blazing headache feeling very ill indeed, I had to go to bed to recover. "Never again" I said to myself.

She rescued some information of the session from memory; the project was typed up for presentation and I was given a copy. When I read it, I just could not relate to it. I vividly remember saying to myself "that's not what I do". On that day I did promise myself that I would not allow anyone else to "examine" me, as far as I was concerned this is me, I have this gift, yes it is fascinating but it is not earthly. I felt that day as though someone had dissected my soul – performed a post mortem on me whilst I was still alive.

I want to tell you very simply how the Spirits communicate, they use the five senses that most of us possess: sight, hearing, feeling, smells and taste. I will describe how each one works giving some examples.

Firstly we deal with clairvoyance, a word familiar to many people but often not understood. The word is derived from the French meaning "clear vision". Because a person is clairvoyant this doesn't necessarily mean that the person using it is a medium. They may be psychic; it's an aid or work tool. I have had many in depth conversations with other mediums and psychics and have made the discovery that we are as individual in the way we work, as we are in the way we look. I have a set of symbols, which are shown, these rely on my intuition, skill and experience to make accurate translations for my clients. Most of the time this is very straightforward. I give to the client what I see; it may be a house, a person, or a place. These could connect to the past, the now or the future. I want to point out, it is never as simple as I am making it sound, but for the sake of this book I am keeping everything very simple.

The images range from rather filmy black and white pictures, to vividly coloured ones. They sometimes resemble a painting or photograph, with these images I often just describe what I see. It is quite a thrill to see a moving picture, best described as watching a video. Some describe a place where an incident has happened in the past; in other cases the event is in the future and is something that the client would find useful to know. I have seen some clairvoyant pictures that have been so mesmerising and magical that I have said out loud "I wish you could see this!" The pictures are seen mainly inside my head but on occasions they leap out in front of me (projected clairvoyance). Only this week whilst doing some work for a client I experienced such powerful clairvoyance. Half the image was inside my head and half was out in front of me, as though the picture - and therefore the message it brought - was important, larger than life.

Let's move on to clairaudience, meaning, "clear hearing". I feel the most famous clairaudient medium of our time must be Doris Stokes. Clairaudience is associated more with mediumship than with psychic experience.

As always I can only describe my own experiences of clairaudience, this however is not my primary work tool. From feedback I discover that hearing sounds and voices does fascinate people, more so than clairvoyance. This tends to be the area that the sceptics (in my experience usually made up of people who are afraid or lack knowledge of this area of life) focus in on. For many people hearing voices in the head does associate with mental illness such as schizophrenia. I know very little about such conditions so find it very difficult to comment, what I know for sure is that I am not mentally ill. I, like many people at some stage in their life, have suffered periods of depression; during those times I had always found it impossible to work with Spirits. The only voice in my head has been the part of protector; encouraging me to climb out of the "dark hole" I have fallen into and, to me, that is my helper. So for me voices in my ear are associated with health and well-being, not illness and depression.

The art of working with voices and sounds is far easier than using any of the other methods of communication; but maybe I am just lazy. They do say "lazy Libran"! It is just that it's very simple, one just repeats what one hears, passing on the name of a loved one in Spirit, or a relevant person on the earth, sometimes it's a full sentence and occasionally it is a whole story.

On one occasion I was doing a sitting, I heard a loud peal of bells. I passed this on to my client along with the words "you must be going to a really special occasion, because the thing that accompanies the bells is beautiful". She replied immediately "I'm getting married next week" it would have been easy to have shown me a "picture" of the wedding, but on this day they chose to communicate using my spiritual auditory system. The location of the voices or sounds that I hear whilst doing a sitting does vary. There are times when they are outside my head, usually behind my ear. The right one is used for earthy matters, the left one for spiritual ones (don't ask me why - I don't know). At other times, though rarely, they are inside my head or body. Very occasionally they are behind me or come from another part of the room. The latter occurs if a communication is a personal message for me, not part of a sitting. Many have been the time when "someone" has shouted my name from upstairs or from another room. I have rushed off to find out who wanted me, only to find no one called or the house was empty. I'm sure many of you recognise this!

My primary channel of communication is clairsentience, describing feelings - the sensing and "knowing" of information. Of all the methods of communication this one is the most difficult to describe; yet I feel there isn't really a need. All of us experience it in a mild form from time to time. The familiar sayings such as "I have a gut feeling" or "I can feel it in my water" are simple yet accurate ways to describe clairsentience. How many of us are truly startled when the "feelings" become reality? I get amused when the sceptical souls among us use these statements. The one person to come to the front of my mind is my father, Henry. When he was on the earth he used this kind of statement yet he professed to live by the script, "When you're dead, you're dead". He was probably the most intuitive and psychic person I have known. I am going to tell you much more about him later - talk about a change of heart!

Clairsentience is a lot more finely tuned than a gut feeling; I usually receive my information in my stomach area (solar plexus). It is there that I receive the information that must be translated and passed on to my client. When a person who is having the reading, or one who connects to the person having their reading, is ill or will be ill, I feel the pain or discomfort in that part of my body, this happens also if a Spirit person is letting me know how they physically died. As soon as I have relayed the message to the client the pain stops.

My least favourite "feelings" are those, which describe how a person passed to Spirit after a long and painful illness such as cancer. A splendid example of such a case was, a lady who came to see me a number of years ago, she was in the process of making major life decisions, and she was finding the challenge an extremely difficult task. Suddenly there was the presence of a Spirit lady in the room, she told me she was my clients mother; soon I was consumed by a pain in my chest and across my back. This was so horrendous that I needed to stand up and grip the edge of my dining table. I could not speak for a while, as the pain was so great. I felt myself rocking as I hung my head down on to my chest in hope that it would help to relieve the pain, but it wouldn't stop. After a few minutes, I raised my head and faced my client, firstly to apologise, but as I looked at her she too was speechless. Tears were rolling down her face and she muttered, "that's my mum, that is what she used to do to ease her pain near the end of a life, she was in so much pain she had to hold on to the table and rock to ease it".

It did take a short while for the pain to ease, then I was able to sit down and commence passing on the deeply personal messages to my client. When that was complete, I asked the lady whether her mum had passed with cancer? "Yes" she replied, "it was a combination of asbestosis and tumours" I had to tell my client that my experience had been "bloody awful". My client explained that the end of her mum's life was "bloody awful" and how relieved she felt for her mum and for herself when it was all over. She proceeded to thank me for providing the evidence that had reinforced an already strong belief that her mum had lived on.

I decided to include this account of working with Clairsentience because it is amongst the most intense spiritual experiences I have had, during the many years of doing this job. This account describes extreme pain but I have also felt this much intensity working with feelings of joy and pleasure and, more importantly, love. I have felt this in its most intense and pure form, virtually impossible to describe, however I will try.

One day I opened my door to a wonderful gentleman called Bill; I invited him in and requested he make himself comfortable. The reading revealed that he had been widowed for some years and that he had resigned himself to the fact that he would spend the rest of his life alone. He still felt a burning, intense love for his wife even though she had been in the Spirit world for ten years. He confided in me the fact that he had believed that he could never be free to love another woman; commitment and marriage were for life!

As the reading unfolded I discovered that a lady had now come into his life, he had, notwithstanding a struggle, fallen in love with her. His problem was that he was consumed with guilt, he felt he was betraying his first wife, Ellen and he simply couldn't handle the complicated emotions he was experiencing.

From my corner, as the medium, the feelings connected to this situation were incredible. I had a feeling all through my body, best described as a crystal clear waterfall, cascading from my head to my toes; the feeling was warm and gentle yet intensely exciting and powerful. This was Ellen's love for Bill, still alive and strong, I described it to him and he became tearful - so did I. There were some moments, which felt like mild electricity was flowing through my body, especially in my fingers and toes. Bill told me this is how their love was, very passionate both physically and mentally. She had been a very erratic, unpredictable lady in life, she had died very suddenly - "unpredictable as usual" he said. Then the whole mood changed, I had a feeling of warmth in my stomach, I could "see" red roses everywhere. Inside me was a "mushy marshmallow" feeling with tingling down my spine. I described this to Bill, where there had been tears in his eyes, his face changed, it became quite red, and he was blushing like an embarrassed schoolboy. "Yes" he said, "I recognise those feelings, that is exactly how it is with Mary" (the new lady in his life) "she's a hopeless romantic and so am I".

The messages given to me from Ellen were that he must get on with his life; he had her blessing. He must consider himself a very lucky man to be so loved by two women, one in the Spirit world and one on the earth, the best of both worlds! Ellen ended the reading by saying her love would never die.

Smells and tastes are experienced rarely in comparison to the primary methods of communication. When Spirits give me smells, they usually make me smile. Many of our Spirit friends have an "off track" sense of humour. On more than one occasion I have had my house filled with the pungent smell of boiling cabbage. On one occasion when this occurred I described to my client what I could smell, she didn't have a trace of this in her nose, however, she did recognise the smell and it connected to her Nan. She told me, when she was a child she would often visit and the house would "stink of cabbage", she would boil it for hours until it was tasteless and resembled a pile of green mush, afterwards the smell would linger all day. Only when my client left the house did the smell go. This is something very simple, but sometimes all that's needed for a person to feel connected or reassured.

Another favourite with the Spirits is the subject of toilets or incontinence! I put this down to the feeling that they are now above all "those things". Being more serious, for many of us having to nurse a relative of friend at the end of their physical life, which involves dealing with toiletries and tending to their intimate needs leaves us with "anchors" which can be triggered at the drop of a hat. White enamel buckets and that smell of Dettol have cropped up on numerous occasions over the years. Regardless of the fact that, in years gone by, more people cared for their sick and elderly relatives at home, detail like this is very commonplace but when it is given it can have quite an impact on the people who are left to tell the tale.

Tastes are less common than smells in readings; nevertheless they are often very meaningful. This is a prime example of the use of taste in spiritual communication. Very early in my career when I considered myself to be inexperienced, I was waiting for my client to arrive, a gentleman, whom I hadn't met before. I walked into my kitchen to put the kettle on, when I suddenly became aware of a "funny taste" in my mouth, next it spread down my windpipe. At first I was puzzled, then I just knew it was the taste of anaesthetic. This taste remained with me until the gentleman arrived for his reading. After greeting him and asking him to sit down and make himself comfortable, I told him about the anaesthetic taste in my mouth. "Good God!" He replied. "I've recently had a heart bypass operation". As soon as he acknowledged this, the taste went from me.

I hope I have been able to "let you in" to this very magical world of spiritual communication and psychic experience. As I said at the start of this chapter, we are all unique. This is just how it is for me; I can't speak for any other mediums.

Chapter Four

Doing the job.

In the last chapter we discussed the two much-asked questions, "how do you know?" and "what does it feel like" this has prompted me to look back on all the questions that I would frequently ask myself throughout the years. The most prominent question being "why do I do this job?" I knew there were many, much easier ways of making a living, so why? The answer was always very simple it was the one I came to every time - because I love people. I knew, from many varied experiences that I have encountered and lived through to tell the tale, what it was like to need someone to talk to on a spiritual or philosophical level. I also knew what it was like to suffer the emotional pain of loss and, last but not least, I needed guidance for the future. So here I was, with a natural gift to help people solve their life's problems and give them some comfort after a bereavement or tragedy, it also meant I could work closely with people so fulfilling my need in that department, "killing two birds with one stone".

Every person that knocked on my door brought with them a unique set of problems or concerns, as individual as the people themselves, everyone needed a different combination of things from me. This always reminded me of years ago when I was a child. One would visit the chemist shop and ask for a "potion", the chemist would proceed to gather ingredients, mix them all up and hand the mixture over the counter in hope that it would alleviate the problem or the symptoms. This is very much how I see my job, - Spiritual advice acting as "preventative medicine". I am a great believer in prevention being better than cure.

I have been so lucky in the enormous amount of feedback I have received from my clients over the years. Without this feedback I know I would not have carried on doing this job. The comments were so helpful that they certainly spurred me on, knowing that the predictions or advice offered from the Spirit world had been proven so right or the advice offered helped people attain their goals or solve their problems, just made it all so worthwhile. This job like most jobs has its ups and downs and there have certainly been times when I wanted out. The whole thing got too much and made me ask, "What's it all about?" I considered this as "hitting the bottom" and this was the point when I decided enough was enough. I would "close shop" - or so I thought. The phone would always ring or a knock would come on the door - a voice would say "can you help me" or words to that effect - how could I refuse, especially feeling that my role in life was to help people. Alternatively it would be a client, calling to give me the outcome of a reading. Some of these results were life transforming.

I have in my mind, dozens of examples. The one that comes to mind above all the rest, at the moment, concerns a lady called Gill; she was ill and was to attend the hospital that very week to undergo tests.

She told me that for a number of weeks she had been suffering and as a result of this, had convinced herself that she had cancer. A few years previously her mother had died of this dreadful disease; this has since been her dread. She may follow in her mother's footsteps, now that dread had turned into fear.

As the sitting preceded the Spirits told me of her fear, which I relayed to Gill, then they said, there was a very real problem which would be detected, through her having the tests, then she would get sorted out. They did however emphasise the importance of the tests then they reassured her that she was not going to pass over to Spirit yet, not now or in the foreseeable future. Gill has been a regular client ever since, so I've got a detailed account of the outcome. There was a small growth which was benign, that was removed and she returned to good health - the whole episode was extremely minor in comparison to the disease from which she was convinced she was suffering.

This is one of the reasons that have kept me from "throwing in the towel". Being able to see outcomes for people, which give them the strength to carry on and face a situation.

My own grandfather took his own life before I was born. He had an ulcer on his leg which he was convinced was a cancer, rather than go through the tests and face the "horrible truth", he decided to end his life. If he had been told by a medium that there was no cancer, it would have allowed him many more years of life. After his death, tests proved it was an ulcer not a cancer.

We all have days when we get out of bed and think, "I would do anything rather than work today". I am no exception; as most people do, I have forced myself to carry on. Amazingly so for me some of these days have brought with them a hidden surprise or reward. Either I have had an outstanding spiritual experience or the sitting has revealed information that has had a profound effect on me personally. Some of these I will share with you throughout the book, needless to say I have always found out, from the feedback that I receive, that it had been well worth my while putting my professional head on.

I am not sure why this is happening, but as I have just been scanning my memory banks, which must hold details from thousands of sittings, I am confronted with the memory of my very first professional sitting.

It was a pleasant September afternoon; I was pacing the floor and feeling "as sick as a dog". Just waiting for the lady who had replied to an advertisement I had placed in my local journal to knock on the door. I remember feeling a "bag of nerves" and being tempted not to be at home, just not answering the door. Whilst I was developing my gift I did lots of sittings for family and friends, suddenly this was a whole new ball game.

26

The hours leading up to this two o'clock appointment had been agony, that morning I regretted ever placing the advertisement. When a knock came on the door at 5 minutes to 2 I realised this was it, there was no way out, I had to step forward and get on with it - it felt like stepping into the unknown.

When I opened the door to this absolute stranger, I saw the look on her face, which made me feel that she was more scared than I was - it made me feel a little easier. I greeted her, took per to the dining room, sat her down and that was it, my first professional sitting was underway. The whole event went very well, she could understand what I was talking about, although I recall it was like "double Dutch" to me. The Spirits used mainly clairvoyance as a mode of communication. It was exciting for me; I had doubted this would work to command – but it did!

I think that day taught me my first and most valuable lesson - the reading is for the client, not for me. No matter how silly, obscure or trivial the information that I receive may be, I have to relay it to my client, it is for them not me, I am just the messenger.

One example of "trivial" detail I was once given, and almost left out of the reading was "a bottle of brown sauce". It seemed silly to me but I did pass it on, I couldn't understand why, if there was a hidden message, I couldn't fathom it out. When I told my client what I could see a bottle of HP sauce, she became quite emotional, she told me that one tea time her mum and dad had sat down to eat their meal. Her dad was not very well at the time so he was eating his food off a tray because he was more comfortable in the armchair. When her mother returned from her journey to the kitchen, armed with the bottle of sauce, she found her dad slumped forward in the chair. He had died very quickly and quietly of a heart attack - so a simple detail like a bottle of brown sauce was a relevant and reassuring detail to this client.

What sorts of people have readings? Just about every sort of person, they come from all walks of life, the richest to the poorest, and the illiterate to the highly academic, male and female, from 16 to 86 (my oldest client). I see lots of adverts in the personal columns that read "clairvoyant readings, female clients only". I understand why people do this; it's a safety precaution. If I had only read for women, I would feel my job was very unfulfilled. I have always enjoyed reading for male clients, they are so interested, there's no half measures with them 99% are already believers, before they set foot over the doorstep, however many have never discussed their belief with another soul just in case they are ridiculed. Nothing about having a reading is light-hearted to men; they always get very involved. The respect they have always shown me as a woman and as a professional has impressed me, not that I am saying I don't get such feelings from my lady clients, because I almost always have - they are great, I have been very lucky. At the end of the day I have only received back what I have given out to clients, respect of people and understanding.

Traditionally readings and séances has been female territory. I have always admired every man who has had the courage or the inclination to set foot into this fascinating world, with a willingness to learn and to "know" about the future or the past, plus the Spirits.

A friend once asked me who my most "unlikely" client had been, by that he meant, the last person on earth anyone thought would have a reading. I thought for a few moments, then one man came clearly into my mind, a giant of a man, standing 6 foot four inches tall, broad shouldered, a very rugged complexion. He was wearing a thick dark overcoat, which made him look much broader than he was. I noticed around his eyes were two dark rings; he looked as though he had been too generous with mascara and it had smudged! In fact he was a coal miner, he came to see me just after he had completed a 6 am to 2 pm shift at the local colliery. I asked him in, as we entered the dining room he took some money out of his pocket and threw it onto the mantelpiece, he said in a very broad Lancashire accent "Reet g'ron wee it luv" (right get on with it love). This I did and the reading flowed beautifully. He was a very gentle character, who was willing to receive spiritual messages. He told me he was very happy with the reading, and then he left as abruptly as he had arrived.

As I said, my clients have come from all walks of life. Manual workers, the unemployed, teachers, the medical profession, the legal profession and, believe it or not, the police - although I'm sure no one would admit it! I could go on and on, what I am really saying is, people, wonderful people, each with an individual story and a unique set of beliefs - how could anyone get bored with a job like this!

My oldest client has got to be a superb lady called Maud, now in the Spirit world. For many years she came to see me and was always accompanied by her daughter, whom she adored, Joan.

The first time Joan came to me for a sitting after Maud's physical death, we were both absolutely delighted that Maud joined us, bringing us some wonderful evidence of her spiritual survival. Firstly we worked our way through some preliminary greetings and details so that we would be in no doubt it was she. Then she moved on to more profound matters, she told us she had been reunited with her first love, her soul mate, who had been in the Spirit world for a number of years. They had met as teenagers, fallen in love and had then parted due to circumstances, not choice. Each had married other people and to be truthful had spent a lifetime regretting their actions. Maud showed me a beautiful Spirit ring, they were now together and she said it had been worth the wait also that the lost time didn't matter.

I thought I had known Maud very well, but I didn't know this. Joan filled me in with more detail, she was aware of the relationship of course, a lot more was said during the sitting. At the end, Joan told me she had been given all the evidence she needed to reinforce her already strong belief that her mum had survived "death".

There used to be a common belief that spiritual matters were for old people, a group of wizened old ladies sitting around a fire reading teacups for even more old ladies. It's just not true, I have found it a struggle looking back over my career to find examples to give you from our more senior citizens. Most of my clients have been aged 30 to 60; however, I do have a very fond memory of one client. He was a gentleman in his seventies. When I opened my door, I found him clutching a small brown fur object in his hand. I asked him in and took him through to the dining room. I was feeling very curious about the object, before we even sat down; he spurted the words "is Isabel here?" The object was a brown fur bonnet that she used to wear in the winter, quite clearly a treasured possession. My response was a tearful one; the love in this man's voice as he spoke her name, touched my heart. I am very pleased to tell you that the Spirit of Isabel was with us that day. She was an excellent communicator, giving proof of a spiritual existence and various personal and loving messages. He told me he was then off to the seniors citizen's luncheon club and felt he would be able to enjoy that meal more than he had enjoyed a meal since she had passed on, a couple of years earlier.

For me there was a strong sensation that he had arrived at the house a lonely soul but he wasn't leaving alone, as if they had re-connected during the reading.

The feelings of loss and grief are more difficult to deal with the older we get. For many people, old age is the lonely end of life, gone it seems are the days of Family Support, everyone is busy "getting on". The sense of family and community seem to have all but disappeared. So when an older person is bereaved, the feeling of emptiness is harder to deal with than if we were younger, say being 17 as opposed to 70. I feel that if a person decides to have a sitting and they received a few comforting words that can ease that dreadful feeling of emptiness inside them, then I feel I have done my job.

The same friend who asked me the question "what kind of people come and see you?" also asked me "why do they come and see you?" "What a big question", I thought. I paused for a moment and answered "because of everything, because of life". He raised his eyebrows as if to say "what a big answer". It is a big answer, for many people life as a whole or part of life, is so difficult, we need something more than maybe a friend's advice - assuming we have friends. A reading highlights another dimension to that problem which can provide an answer, a solution or simply bring hope. There are people who appear to flow through life effortlessly but who will almost inevitably experience a trauma at some stage in their life, usually later rather than sooner. This may be a loss or an illness, just some event that they feel incapable of handling alone.

Much too many people's surprise, bereavement is the least likely reason that prompts a person to book a sitting. Remember that I can only talk for myself here. Some other mediums specialise in dealing with the bereaved. I am not saying this is never the reason for people coming to me for a reading. I do seem to specialise in earthly problems such as relationships, finance, work and family issues. If I were pushed, I would say the highest reason on the list is decision-making.

Not everyone is looking for an easy answer or a quick fix; they rarely get that even though I have known it to be possible on occasions. They want some insight, either into the future or into a situation around them at that time or direction and spiritual advice. There is more on offer than a "quick fix". Many people come for predictions, these I do, I don't deny it, although they are scattered throughout the reading and aren't always clear at the time. Sometimes there aren't any predictions included in a reading but only on very rare occasions. I have always told my clients "I can only give what I get" I'm not a magician or a fortune-teller. I'm a spiritual helper. Sometimes I feel like a bridge, sometimes I feel like a teacher or adviser, but almost always I feel like a friend to people.

Chapter Five

Psychic / Spiritual

As I mentioned earlier, there were a variety of reasons for writing this book, however, I have left out.what may be the primary reason, the word sharing. Even though I'm really enjoying writing the book I do find it a difficult task. I have to deal with a lot of internal conflict. One side of me wants to open up and share myself and the knowledge stored in my mind, and that is very public. The other side of me is the part that has always been very private about both my work and myself. I never wanted to seek "fame" or public acknowledgement. Initially working within the four walls of my dining room and for the last few years using written communication, just helping people and earning a modest living doing something I feel is worthwhile has been enough for me,

So you can imagine the "war" that went on, when the time came to sit down and write the book. Even though I always said I would do it, when it came to it, I had to overcome this obstacle. I knew if I decided to tell my story it would mean changing my pattern and I didn't know how that would suit my character.

Well it is obvious which part of me won the battle, but then I said to myself "there are enough famous medium's and books on mediumship, did the world need another one?" I searched within for the answer and it came back "yes". My story is mine, no better or worse than anyone else's, it is worth telling, everyone is worthy of a hearing I always tell myself. I have read some marvellous spiritual books; some are quite technical others are packed with famous names. I can't pack mine full of famous names, because apart from one well-known sportsman, whom I will mention in a moment, this book is about ordinary yet very special people. When anyone has met as many people as I have on a very emotionally, intimate level, it doesn't take along to realise just how many special people there are in this world.

The sportsman I mentioned is ex-Leeds rugby player Neil Harmon, I say ex because heaven knows whom he will be playing for when this book is published. I mentioned Neil because during one sitting I did for him, I promised him that I would, but more so because he fits into the category of those "unlikely" to have a reading. He is yet another gentle giant of a man with a strong spiritual belief. He has used spiritual guidance to help build his very successful career in the highly competitive world of sport. He told me that spiritual advice has been "a mentor" whilst he has been making important decisions regarding his career and personal affairs.

I have always been a bit of a loner where mixing with other people in this profession has been concerned. I have found an awful lot of snobbery and prejudice amongst fellow mediums. I first encountered it early on in my career; this is what made me become a loner where work was concerned. I want to explain that there are two levels or methods of working, one being on a spiritual level, the other a psychic level.

Here are the dictionary definitions of each.

Psychic: -   Outside the possibilities determined by natural laws. Sensitive to forces not recognised by natural laws.

Spiritual: -   Relating to the Spirit or soul and not physical nature or matter. Believing that the disembodied Spirits of the "dead" survive in another world and can communicate with the living in this world.

Many people have psychic experiences; in fact it is possible to train your mind to become more open or aware of psychic and spiritual happenings. All over the country there are people who run development groups, often they are connected to spiritualist churches, some are privately run. They are open to people who want to develop their already high intuitiveness or want to become more spiritually aware.

I was a psychic a long time before I became a medium. I'm not quite sure, but I feel that sitting in a development circle is a way of demanding mediumship. This sounds like a criticism of development groups, it isn't; I just feel from my own development, that mediumship isn't something that can be demanded. In recent years I feel that psychic development is possible for most people who are prepared to make the effort, this can be the "gateway" to spiritual development, mediumship.

When I was growing up, from time to time, I would "feel" or "know" things were going to happen, very much a "flash in the pan" situation, years apart sometimes. Almost everyone I have known and who has spoken freely on this subject has experienced this "knowing" on occasions. It can be a dream or a feeling, or even a daydream, it can be wonderful or very distressing for the recipient, what is clear is the fact that it happens to people all the time.

I can't explain it I don't want to. I just except it, as I wish more people would. I do feel generally in life there is a grave lack of acceptance. If we could take people and situations as they are, we would all be able to get on a lot better and faster. We seem to feel we have to get to the bottom of everything. Prove or disprove things and make changes. Fooling ourselves that the changes are for the better, not always so and I feel that there will be many questions left unanswered in this life. It is only when we get to the Spirit world we will then learn the answers.

34

To explain the "spiritual" is very simple, it's as the dictionary definition states, in a nutshell the Spirit of a "dead" person communicating with the Spirit of a living person. I talked about snobbery amongst mediums, there are those who feel, and are not afraid to voice their views, that it is beneath them to work with a client at a psychic level, as though it were for amateurs.

I don't choose how I work, I get what is given and I'm very grateful. The combination of the spiritual and psychic can be a magical mix. I know I have done many sittings on a purely psychic level and that has worked very well. I have always maintained that I am only the messenger! "It's not for me to question why, but to do".

As a medium, when I see the future for someone else it can be both fascinating and frightening. Being psychic enables one to "see" or "feel" what lies ahead. What situations, events, even people are waiting on the road ahead? People are advised about these important details in hope that they may have something to aim for or look forward to, things that are outside their normal fields of vision. It may be that some things would best be avoided; if that isn't possible then there is time to prepare for such events, such as for a death. I was forewarned of the passing of both my parents, a few months ahead of each. I didn't like it, but it gave me time to prepare mentally. It was as though a cushion had been placed behind me so that when the time came I would not fall onto a hard floor, but onto the soft cushion. I have to say it worked well; it was better to know what to expect rather than to be taken by surprise then crash to the ground emotionally. My friend Sylvestro "lost" his mother in July 1997. There was no word of warning, he was devastated, for him there was no preparation time, no chance to say goodbye, it makes me realise just how lucky I was, having time to prepare. In the past a large number of my clients have said the same, the forewarning was difficult to accept, but proved to be a "God send".

Working with clients at a spiritual level gives us the evidence that so many others are constantly searching for or need. Reinforced belief that life carries on after "death"; there is a transition from physical life to spiritual life. This can be so difficult for we "earthlings" to understand, but the Spirits try their best to educate us. Until the time we go to the Spirit world ourselves, I'm sure we will only know or understand a little.

Mediums have Spirit guides that help them to do their job. Just as people need to see a medium who will translate and pass the messages on from the Spirit world, the same can apply especially for new Spirits. They don't have the energy or know how to do it themselves, so they use a Spirit guide. To be light hearted for a moment I do wonder how some messages get through because by the time it's been passed from

35

the Spirit to the guide to the medium and on to the client its fourth hand!

Apart from being messengers and interpreters, Spirit guides teach philosophy, give guidance and direction. I do enjoy doing readings that are a combination of the psychic and spiritual. I feel this gives the reading different dimensions and includes the past, the present and the future. For many clients this can prove to be truly valuable and life enhancing.

Chapter Six

Children and animals.

I'm sure most of us are familiar with the show business rule "never work with children or animals". Some mediums specialise in working with Spirit children such as the late Doris Stokes; she seemed to be a magnet for them. I once heard of a medium, I know her name is Pat and she used to live in the Congleton area of Cheshire. Her speciality was helping people to locate their lost animals in the event they had passed to the Spirit world, in some cases this lady could communicate with lost pets, absolutely marvellous, for the grieving owners.

My speciality has always seemed to be a "magnet" for forgotten souls. People who have "died" and been forgotten or that physical death was so long ago, their memory has faded or there is no one alive who really remembers them. I know it has set many people on the road to research their family tree, just in case anyone else "pops up" in a future reading. A very long time ago I was given the name Isabella in Spirit, it meant nothing to me. A recent look at the 1881 census revealed that Isabella was my great grandmother on my father's side of the family.

I have been lucky to experience some extraordinary spiritual communications with both animals and children, which have remained clearly in my mind and are very treasured.

I did a sitting, many years ago now, for a client called Ann-Marie and this was a good general sitting. We covered many subject areas, relationships, finance, children and so on. I have to say I get on very well with most of my clients and this lady was no exception. Time passes very quickly when I'm doing a sitting, so it's difficult to say just how long it was into the sitting before there was a drastic change in the atmosphere of the room, this was brought about by the tremendously strong presence of what felt to be a "childlike" Spirit. I knew it was female and the only way to describe this presence is of someone flitting around the room, as if they were playing with me. I sensed fast movement, first at one side of the room, then at the other. I was confused and felt teased.

I didn't have a clairvoyant picture at this time, however, I did have a voice in my ear saying "Mitzie" and the voice was female and young. I automatically presumed Anne-Marie had lost a child, and today she wanted to make contact.

"Do you know Mitzie?" I asked, at first there was a long silence, as I looked at the lady's face I could see her eyes were filled with tears, she was choked with emotion. Then her voice emerged from all of this and she proclaimed "its Mitzie it's my dog!" I was able to tell her that Mitzie's Spirit was still around, she had progressed in Spirit life and she now had a voice. Her personal message to her "mother" was one of deep love and affection, undying love.

This experience was one of sheer delight for me. I did get the feeling that the communication for Ann-Marie was more of a shock than a pleasure - at least at first. She had come for a sitting, very open minded and expected any of a number of Spirits to come through, but never in her wildest imaginings did she expect it to be Mitzie - her dog!

Mitzie is only one of a large number of contacts I have had with Spirit animals, including cats, dogs, a budgie and a horse.

Kate came to see me as she was going through a very distressing time in her life. Her marriage had collapsed, her life felt in tatters, she had lost all of her self-esteem and as she put it, she was "going around and around in circles". The reading revealed a lot of detail for Kate, but at that moment I felt I had no words of hope neither could I "see" any pathway forward.

Then I felt burdened with a huge sense of guilt, I wondered, what that was all about, but I didn't mention it's at that stage. Soon things started to link together. In the midst of the feelings of emotional strain, I had with me the Spirit of a horse. My voice changed, it deepened and it didn't sound like me, I made a vane attempt to clear my throat, but that was useless. Next I could feel a sharp pain in my lungs, especially across my back, my throat became sore and, I know this will sound ridiculous, but my head felt as though it was swelling, it felt (even though it wasn't) enormous, like a horse's head.

Next the auditory messages started to flow, his voice just sounded like that of a man with a very deep voice, very strong and noble. He was very eager for Kate to know that, before he passed to Spirit, she had done everything possible for him and it was his time to enter the Spirit world, nothing could have prevented that. He asked if she would help him by carrying on loving him in the Spirit world as she had done on the earth, as you can imagine this was a very emotional time for both of us, we both shed tears.

I want to explain that whilst Kate was going through the emotional strain of a marriage break-up, her horse had become sick. He developed pneumonia and had to be put to sleep. The guilt I felt with Kate was her blaming herself for her horse's death. She felt she had been so involved with her own problems that she missed all the warning signs when her "lad" - the name that she called him - started with pneumonia. She therefore felt to blame for the illness and his death. The horse wanted her to know this would have happened anyway, she must not blame herself.

Kate has been a regular visitor to me for sittings since that first emotive meeting. On a second visit she told me that the messages from her horse had helped her to create a turning point in her life. Her "lad's" words helped to ease the pain, from then on, she found herself gathering strength, which had helped her to think clearly, make decisions, and then act upon them. The results had been that she had rebuilt her life, personally and career wise. Following a job and house move, she had ventured into pastures new and, most importantly, she had been able to dump the guilt she had carried since her horse had become ill and died. She had been able to grieve for her "trusted friend", now able to open her heart and let the spiritual love from him fill it, this had given her more strength to live her life.

"Letting go" of our loved ones, once they have passed to Spirit, is very, very, difficult for many of us. I have grieved as deeply, and in some cases, more deeply, for animals that I have lost than for certain people. Often people say "it's only a dog" or "cat", it isn't the "package" that determines whom or what is worthy of our sadness and grief, it is the relationship that was formed whilst the person or animal was on the earthly plane.

Even with all the knowledge of spiritual matters that I have accumulated over the years plus a deep belief that life transcends earthly death, I too, like numerous people that I have met during my lifetime, have at times found great difficulty in accepting or coming to terms with certain "deaths". I always told myself I must accept it, because of the job I do, after many years of struggling with this rule or demand, I had to give in and except the fact that at the end of the day I'm only human and some things can be too hard to take!

My mum, Annie, passed to Spirit in 1986 after a 19 year battle with cancer, I was struggling emotionally; I just couldn't find the comfort I needed from anyone or anywhere. Then the words that Kate's horse had given to her, as she struggled with her mixed emotions, came flooding back to me, "I must open my heart to the Spirit's love, let it fill my heart in order that I may heal", in turn aiding my mum's spiritual progress. It took quite a while, but it really worked.

I must share with you details of a sitting that I had, myself, some years ago. The medium said to me "I have Peter in the Spirit world with me. He liked to wear blue clothes, he was very small in stature but I feel he had plenty to say for himself". Peter was my budgie, yes he was blue and small in stature, and yes he did have a lot to say for himself. When I was given this information it really made me smile, as it is now, at this moment of writing, I hope it has made you smile!

Spiritual experiences with animals are very commonplace; it's just that, for some reason people tend to dismiss them as irrelevant. Apart from gathering information during sittings, lots of clients and friends have shared their experiences with me and I feel very privileged.

A very close friend of mine, Jenny, who passed to Spirit in 1995, shared with me many funny or amazing stories of Spirit visits and premonitions, which concerned animals. For a considerable number of years she, along with the help of her husband and daughter, ran a boarding kennel and cattery, plus an animal rescue in North

41

Staffordshire. As an animal lover, she was a hopeless case. When it came to parting with some of these rescued animals, her "special cases" as she called them, the relationships were so strongly developed, that many never got to be re-homed, they found a permanent home with Jen. It was strange how things worked out, but most of the "rescues" that she kept, ended up living extremely long lives. With some of these animals, the friendship was so deep that an element of telepathy developed. She told me "they mentally talked to her" and she responded. With certain of them she described relationships as spiritual, she felt she had met the Spirits of some animals before, maybe in a different life. They may have returned to her through the rescue to finish some business. I love that train of thought; I just believe it because it makes me feel warm and nice inside.

When the life of one of her animals, whether it was a rescue or one of the many Dalmatians that she bred, was coming to an end, preceding this event she would almost always have a Spirit visitor. Very often it would be the last animal that had passed to Spirit. These visitors quite often were in a solid form and, to use her words, would "shock the hell out of me". The phone would ring in my home, it would be Jenny saying "I have seen 'such a body' today", we looked on this as the official warning. Sometimes she was nursing a sick dog so she was expecting a passing, but not always, so there would still be a lot of shock around the passing, all that she knew was there would be "one less". The forewarning did help to lessen the shock, and gave her time to mentally prepare for another "parting of the ways".

As you can gather, with such a menagerie to care for, animal death and premonitions became a way of life over the years, Jenny wasn't unique with these premonitions and animal Spirit visitors. Sadly many people don't feel that they can tell anyone, their thoughts seem to be that it's risky enough disclosing that they have seen a Spirit person but a Spirit animal! Surely they would be considered eccentric or insane! I have decided to own up, I used to be like that myself, afraid of being labelled for my beliefs and experiences. The decision to write this book is my public exclamation that I don't care anymore! At least not what people think of me where spiritual and psychic matters are concerned! I do hope some of the people who read this will also adopt this attitude and "stand up and be counted", there are so many people out there, who are ready to listen to your experiences and desperate to share theirs with you – believe me.

I have just introduced you to my friend Jenny, Jennifer Gladys Jones to give her full title. I met her in May 1985 and I can honestly say, "Life has never been the same since". It was the purchase of a Dalmatian puppy that brought us together; we saw Jenny's advertisement in the kennel magazine. She lived in Staffordshire, but that proved only a short distance to travel when you consider what I received in return. I bought from her a gorgeous puppy that brought so much joy and learning into my life, plus this was the beginning of ten-year earthly friendship between Jenny and myself.

I named my puppy Jennifer in Jenny's honour. Jenny (Dalmatian) had a short life just six years, an epileptic who became profoundly deaf (I developed sign language in order to communicate) she suffered with

a breakdown of her immune system and eventually developed cancer. She was so brave; I had to care for her as if I was caring for a child. She showed me and taught me so much. In the July of 1991, I knew it was time to "let her go". We too had developed a telepathic form of communication, I knew what she wanted and needed me to do for her, so I responded.

I'm a great believer in people and animals having a "good death" - whenever possible. Tuesday 9th July, I knew this was the day, so I arranged for Mr. Hall, the vet, to come to the house to administer the injection. I acted out of love for her, I wanted to keep her with me forever, but that was selfish. She lay on her favourite settee I had her head in my hands, the needle was slipped into her paw and she slipped away almost as quickly. What I experienced was amazing, I had felt so distressed leading up to this event, and then a deep sense of calm filled my body instantly. I had the sensation of "something" entering my abdomen, then this force working up my body and out of my head; it felt as though a lift was racing through my body, which acted as the lift shaft. I truly believe this was Jenny's Spirit passing through me on its journey to the Spirit world. I was left feeling very calm and very still, I didn't feel a need for tears at that time. This allowed me to do the necessary actions that a situation like this requires one to do.

To many, this was just having my dog put to sleep. To me it felt as though I had just physically lost "my child". Today, as I write, even though it has been years since that happened, if I close my eyes, I can feel that sensation of Jenny's Spirit passing through me, a powerful yet reassuring memory. Even though I have heard a lot of accounts, from friends and clients, about animal Spirits, this one remains unique.

My Jennifer (Jenny Wren to me) passed to Spirit on Tuesday the 9th of July 1991, three days later Friday the 12th I was still so raw with the emotional pain I was feeling, so drained, I felt exhausted. I decided to go to bed early that evenings however sleep wouldn't come, I just lay there. Suddenly there was a loud and clear noise coming from the landing. The noise was very distinctive to me; it was a "rap-rap-rap" as though someone was banging something against the door. At once I sat up in bed to see if I could see anything, but I couldn't. This familiar sound was Jenny letting me know she had arrived in the Spirit world. When she was in her earthly body she would often stand in the doorway to the bedroom, looking at me and she would beat the door or wall with her tail, as with most dogs, this was how she displayed her pleasure. She did it with such gusto that I was always sure she would break her tail off.

I was so delighted, I couldn't think of a better way she could have chosen to let me know that she was OK and to me it was clear she was happy and out of pain. The banging noise was accompanied with a "belly cry", this had always been the way she greeted me if I had left the house and, on occasion, left the room. There had been three extremely sad, empty days since she passed to Spirit, and I felt reconnected with her but the grief continued for a very long time, a lot longer than I care to admit.

A relative of mine has become quite an interesting philosopher of both earthly and spiritual matters. For years she has watched people and gathered information. The three-day gap between Jenny's death and spiritual visit to me reminded her of the Bible. After Christ was put to death the Bible says "on the third day he rose again". She has experienced a number of three-day spiritual events and has had even more people confide a similar experience to her.

Jenny was only six when she past to Spirit, even with all her health problems I felt that was too short a life for such a wonderful creature, however the turn of events which led to her "death" were not a surprise to me. Just a year before she passed to Spirit. I took her on holiday to Dorset; we stayed in a charming cottage in the village of Fiddleford. Prior to the holiday she hadn't been well, with all her health problems I was used to her developing new or unusual symptoms, all "par for the course" I thought, so I didn't worry too much.

As we got further into the holiday, she seemed to get worse, lots of tummy trouble, loss of appetite and she was very quiet, not like her at all. On the Wednesday night I had a very disturbing "dream". In this "dream" a person started hammering on the cottage door. The cottage was in a secluded rural setting, so as I rushed downstairs I was very wary of opening the door. When I did, I was faced with the very weathered face of a farmer, he blocked the doorway with his body, in

44

his hand he held a double-barrelled shotgun, he just shouted at me "Jenny's got cancer". I awoke Instantly, I was sweating, my heart raced and I was feeling very distressed, as I'm sure you can imagine.

I knew this was no ordinary dream, but I didn't want to believe the man in the dream. As soon as I returned from this holiday I took Jenny to see the vet, more so, because the condition had worsened than just because of the "dream". Tests were done; day-to-day she seemed to become more poorly. It was a very long week waiting for the results. I have to admit I "knew" things were not good and these were confirmed by the vet when he told me Jenny had cancer, but of course I had already been told that hadn't I!

This sort of stuff happens all the time to ordinary people, you don't have to be a medium to have a sense of "knowing" or experience premonition dreams. Most are less obvious than this example; often the message is interwoven, if you're asking the question "how do we know when we have had one?" I feel the only answer I can give is, they feel different, and somehow they seem more real.

Our family is like many others, we have owned and cared for some splendid animals over the years and have suffered the pain of grief, when they have had to leave us. In February of 1988 my sister and her family, very unexpectedly, "lost" their treasured dog, Candy, a beautiful golden retriever. They had taken her out for walk and she suddenly collapsed. After being rushed to the vets, tests showed that candy had cancer of the heart. The end of her life came in a few hours; they were devastated. There had been no time to prepare emotionally or physically for this, the loss of their "baby".

Like most animals, Candy had a collection of toys, the favourite of these being a hand knitted teddy called Ted. After Candy's death Ted had been placed, for safety, on top of a tall chest of drawers in my nephew's bedroom. Having two other dogs in the house, she didn't want them to harm Ted in any way, plus they each had their own special toys. Can you imagine the shock, a few days after Candy's "death" when my sister came back into the house and found Ted in the middle of the dining room floor? At first she thought that one of the dogs had managed to get it down, when she investigated, nothing else on the drawers had been disturbed. A dog would've had to leap at the drawers to reach Ted, bringing everything else down with it.

Not knowing what to really think, she sort of left it floating in her mind. All this changed over the next few weeks, when Ted appeared all over the house, on her bed, in the lounge, once in the bathroom and even in the kitchen. This was very reassuring for the family, and it only stopped when my sister spoke to Candy. She told her Spirit "I've got your message Candy, I know you are still around". As far as I know Ted hasn't been moved since that time. This sort of behaviour, I normally associate with Spirit children rather than animals, but at the end of the day, they are all Spirits, which strive the best they can to prove that life continues beyond that of the earthly body.

My ex-husband Michael worked for a small firm of accountants. He spent a lot of time in the office out of working hours. I felt like an accountant's widow, so I spent some evenings there with him, "better than sitting alone at home" I thought. The building was extremely interesting; it had been the Co-operative funeral service for many years and I have to admit the vibes in this place used to "blow my mind" at times.

Often I would wander around the building showing an interest (being nosy!) One particular evening I popped my head into the owner's office, my thoughts were "what a bombsite". Suddenly there appeared the spiritual figure of a young boy; I would age him at between three and five years old. Fair-haired, he wore short grey pants with white knee socks and some sort of pale coloured shirt. He was kneeling on a chair looking out of the window. I just "knew" he was the boss's son. For a long time I didn't feel I could approach my ex-husband's boss with this information, so I just put it to the back of my mind and thought, that was the end of that. As with most firms of accountants, it wasn't very long before a social occasion arose. I was asked along and thankfully, this really was social, all the formalities flew out of the window. Later in the evening, after the drinks had been flowing, this man started to chat to me about his personal life; I was surprised because he was a very private person, protective of personal details. It seemed that a few years earlier he had been in a relationship with a lady who became pregnant. Not feeling committed to the relationship; she had the pregnancy terminated, which ended the relationship. He told me this had happened four years earlier, and he often thought about the child, was it a boy or a girl?

I was faced with a dilemma, should I tell him about the little boy or not? I assessed the situation quickly and carefully then decided not to say anything, the man had drunk a lot but the real reason was that it didn't feel right to do so.

So why have I told you the story? I have been asked the question, "what happens when a person has a termination?" I hope I have just answered your question. The Spirit passes into the Spirit world and grows and progresses as a Spirit child. Exactly the same way babies who have died through natural causes or who were still born or miscarried do. I have had two very early miscarriages, one a boy and the other a girl. I feel reassured that they have been cared for in the Spirit world by Spirit mothers.

Most sittings begin with general information about the client's life; the lady I talk about next was no exception. This sitting took place at the start of my career around 1983'ish. I was chatting away merrily, then I began to cough and cough. I knew this wasn't my problem, this was a Spirit wanting to join us in the sitting and say something, and this was their way of forcing a way in.

I must admit I'm not super woman, when I conduct a sitting I can only deal with one subject or one Spirit at a time. I imagine them in my mind, making an orderly queue, coming forward one at a time. (In the film "Ghost" Whoopi Goldberg's portrayal of Oda-May Brown demonstrates what I mean, in no uncertain terms, she tells them "one at a time and in order please"). Unfortunately it doesn't always work out like this, they just butt in and create a lot of confusion for me. Giving me physical symptoms like the cough is one way of pushing in.

The cough got worse and worse and became a feeling of choking, then of drowning. At first I was rendered speechless, then she spluttered a name - "Dolly, Dolly, I've got someone called Dolly with me". The lady having the sitting started to chuckle and shake her head as if in disbelief. Then she spoke, "it's not Dolly her name wasn't Dolly but I know who she is!" this little girl was a relative and many years ago she had fallen into a dolly tub full of water and had drowned. Upon discovering this, the feeling of drowning ceased. "Thank God" I thought. I went on to apologise for getting mixed up, the lady didn't mind at all. I could "see." her then as a lovely young woman who had grown and matured in the Spirit world. The reason she brought this memory was in order to identify herself, because the lady would not have recognised her now, so often with children, this is how they identify themselves, as they were or how things were at the time they passed, it does not mean that their Spirits' have not blossomed.

Chapter Seven

Suicide.

Suicide is a profoundly emotive word, conjuring up a host of mixed feelings within anyone who has had the remotest dealings with a suicide victim. The views of people who have had no personal encounters, more often than not are extremely judgmental or non-committal. I've never been a stranger to the word or the act. Four members of my family chose to take their own lives and various other members attempted to do so.

I found out what suicide meant when I was just 10 years of age. I was very lucky to have grown up in a lane on the edge of an urban town, Tyldesley in Lancashire. To reach the lane one had to go under a railway bridge and the lane stretched out into fields and farmland. It felt very secluded and safe. We lived at No. 52, at No. 66 lived my aunt Ada, my mum's sister. As a child I adored her, I was born on her birthday the tenth of October, I always felt that made us somehow special to each other.

One day she was talking to me about the family, she really was the authority on our ancestors; she knew almost all there was to know. My grandfather, her father, was the topic of the day. As she talked about him, there was a change in her voice, a kind of disapproval; it's hard when you are child to put these things into words. I just remember the feeling well. This prompted me to ask her "what's happened to granddad, how did he die?" She replied quite coldly and abruptly "he cut his head off!" I emotionally reeled in horror, I was very shocked and have never forgotten the feelings of that moment. I was so upset that I couldn't ask any more questions. I thought it was a terrible thing to say, not that I doubted it to be true, I just knew I was a little girl and you don't say things like that to a little girl!

I carried these dreadful words and the vivid images they created inside my head, around with me for years. I just felt I couldn't talk to mum about this, I knew she would have been upset with my auntie, saying something like "fancy talking to a child like that!" I also felt that if Mum knew, she would fall out with Ada and I would be to blame, so I left it.

When I was a teenager, just 13, we did speak about the whole subject of suicide. In particular my grandfather, it was at this time that I told her what Ada had told me, years earlier. She was appalled and said just as I had expected "fancy telling a child that". Mum followed through with, "this is Ada's way, she either laughs things off or can be very dramatic about anything that deeply upsets her, if she finds some things difficult to handle, she's always been the same." We had no choice, but to forgive her we both loved her.

I felt ready to ask questions about my granddad, or more to the point, hear the truth about his death. Mum explained that my granddad had been depressed for quite some time, due to his concerns

51

about an ulcer on his leg. (As far as we know, that was the reason) As I explained earlier in the book, he thought the ulcer was a cancer, and he just couldn't face a lingering, painful death. So one night when my nana was in bed asleep, he went outside to the toilet with a large kitchen knife, there he cut his own throat. My nana found his body the morning after; obviously the family was devastated.

Granddad was not the only member of mum's family to take their own life, two of her sisters Dorothy and Ruth did also. Mum felt this was a good time to tell me about these other tragedies. Dorothy was mum's oldest sister, when her husband gave his attention to another woman, Dorothy found this intolerable and ended her life by putting her head in a stream and drowning herself.

All this was a lot to absorb; the timing of these details was quite unbelievable, as though Mum was laying the groundwork for the events that were to happen in November that year. Staying with us at that time was my auntie Ruth, she had immigrated to Australia many years earlier with her husband and two young children, this has been before I was born. Ruth returned home to England in June 1965, she was nursing a broken heart, Ron, her husband, had left her for someone else. She couldn't stay in Australia without her beloved Ron, so she came home. I believe she came home to die. One very cold and frosty November evening she announced to Mum that she was going out, this surprised her because Ruth had just been ill, and Mum didn't consider her well enough to go out.

Ruth was strong-minded, she decided she was going and that was that. Just before she left, she stood in the living room for a while dressed in a coat and hat that she had borrowed from my sister, then she said "I'm going now" - she went and never came back. The next morning, my mum alerted the police that Ruth had not returned, they set about searching the area, but it was a man taking an early morning walk along the canal who found her body, floating in the water. It took a few hours for the police to bring the news to our home. I can't describe the grief I felt at that moment. I said "there is no God, he wouldn't let things like this happen", I have learned as I have travelled through my life that we have free will, if we decide to end our life, God can't stop us.

This event and the feelings surrounding it are deeply etched on my mind, obviously this was Ruth's decision and I'm sure it was right for her, just as it was the will of Dorothy and my granddad. Writing this book has made me realise just how much I have "swept my feelings under the carpet" concerning these "deaths" - especially Ruth's. After all, we were all very close; she had shared a bedroom with my sister and me during her short stay with us.

My granddad James Henry, Dorothy, Ruth and my Uncle George who also drowned himself in the local canal are all regular Spirit visitors to other members of the family and to me. This does give me great comfort because of the attitude that society used to have in general, relating to suicide, I say used to have because so much has changed. Suicide is on the increase due to the pressures of life, so it is unfortunately affecting more and more people.

Suicide used to be classed as a criminal offence. The aspect of the act, which concerns many people, is whether it is or is not a crime against God. Different religions have different beliefs about suicide plus the fate of the soul. The Catholic religion has very strong views; people who take their own lives are doomed to purgatory. The last thing I want to do is offend anyone or step on their toes by voicing my own opinions, well it isn't my opinion really it's my findings after working with the relatives of suicide victims for so many years.

Whether a person died of natural causes or they bring their own life to an end, there is a place for everyone in the Spirit world. People who commit suicide are usually very ill physically or mentally. For so many the pressures of life are so great, that they choose this as their best option, they simply lose their will to live. I have heard so many people class suicide victims as cowards; in my mind there is nothing cowardly about putting a knife to one's own throat or jumping in a river. Whatever the method they choose, it takes guts. It is my belief that such Spirits are treated with tender loving care when they reach the Spirit world; they are nursed back to "spiritual health".

Before we go on to share some of my very special spiritual contacts, I would like to tell you it took my grandfather James Henry 35 years before he made contact with anyone in the family. After my sister gave birth to her son in 1984 she suffered a nervous breakdown. This illness went on and on, my sister began to believe she would never be well again. At this time I was at an early stage in my spiritual development. I often did practice sittings for her, which helped us both. It helped me to develop and offered my sister lots of help and comfort. One afternoon I really felt compelled to sit down and relay the message that was being given.

I could "see" a gentleman, mending a pair of shoes on a last; he was attaching a new sole to one of the shoes. At first I didn't understand, nor did I recognise the man. Slowly he turned his head and I recognised him from a photograph my mum had. Then he gave me a message for my sister, I had to tell her that she would be well again, just like the pair of shoes she would mend. He went on to say, she must be patient, and he explained that when he was ill, he would not listen to the doctors. He thought he would never be well, so he took his life. He asked me to ask her, not to consider this path; she was going to mend.

The communication was very clear and powerful, this was my first of many contacts with Spirits who had ended their own lives, but it was so special being my granddad.

I want to tell you about Elsie one of my "veteran" clients. Her visits to me must have spanned a period of 12 years, as with most clients, when life is proving to be very difficult she would visit more often, then when the crisis had passed, there would be a gap until she needed more spiritual guidance and advice.

Apart from her wonderfully pleasant personality, which I still, find extremely rare amongst people these days. The unusual thing about Elsie is that after raising her family to adulthood, she conceived and produced a child in her late '40s called Diane; we will meet her later in the book, as she's quite an exceptional child.

There had been a gap of about three years since Elsie last came to see me, usually a good sign but not in this case. My mouth dropped open when I opened the door. Elsie won't mind me saying that she had been a "large lady", but no more. Standing before me was a very thin lady dressed in a Mackintosh belted at the waist. This was something that I wouldn't have expected Elsie to wear. To my eyes she was just a shadow of the woman I had known. I know now that dieting was highly responsible for the weight loss, but as she entered the house, I could see emotional pain was etched all over her face and I could feel vibrations of pain and loss. I don't have permission to disclose intimate details of this sitting, however I can tell you that Elsie's visit was made in the hope that she would make contact with her son. Just a few months before this visit he had used a leather belt to hang himself in the back garden of his home.

What I really want to share with you is the "happy ending" of this story - but sadly not for the people left behind; it was Elsie's son who wanted us to know how happy he was. Not yet 30 years old, he told me he felt hopeless and helpless when he was in his earthly life. He told me that this was the best way forward for him. He just wanted his mum to try and understand something about his feelings at the time of his passing; however, he asked to be forgiven for the pain he had caused to everyone on the earth. There was great emphasis on the peace he had found and how happy he felt. He asked that she relay this to the people that mattered and also the message that "life really does go on mum".

A lot of information was passed to Elsie through me, which was very personal, but the last message he gave me I'm sure he would want me to put in this book. He told me that he was being well cared for in the Spirit world and wanted his mum to know that "it isn't true what they say about being cast out when you take your own life, it's just not true". He ended with "I feel free!"

54

I had a pre-conception that most people, who killed themselves, did it by taking an overdose of tablets. In my job, I have come across more cases where people have hung themselves. Marilyn's son used to work in our local cotton mill. He was a teenager, seemed to be "full of life", and got on with most people; he gave the appearance of being happy. That is why people were so stunned when he took his own life.

It was just another working day in the mill, people stopped to take their break. When John left the floor, people presumed he had gone to the toilet, so no one thought any more about it. When, after an hour, he hadn't returned, one of his work mates decided to go and look for him. At first there was no luck, then one of the older workers (On instinct I feel) decided to search further. This mill had been closed a little at a time over a number of years, so there were whole floors empty. John was discovered hanging in a stairwell.

Anyone who reads this book and has children, won't find it difficult to imagine the agony that John's mother and Elsie went through, when they discovered what their children felt it was necessary to do to find peace of mind.

Marilyn came to me, distraught; she was blaming herself for what had happened. She had tried to convince herself it had been an accident, and then she tried to convince herself it had just been a cry for help. It took two sittings, a few months apart, before there was any contact from John. He needed to heal spiritually before he was ready or able to make contact. When he did, it was amazing, so very clear I recall. He was very positive and firm in his statements. He wanted me to tell his mum that no one was to blame, least of all her. This wasn't an accident; he intended it to happen. He apologised deeply for the dramatic way he had ended his life and that was his only regret. He said that if he could do it again he would be more discrete, to save everyone's embarrassment and horror.

He repeatedly said to me "I'm happy". Then he asked me to tell his mum not to feel sad for him, he was progressing and he wanted her to do the same, she also had to give this message to the family. He ended his communication by saying he would not want to come back to live in his earthly body and that he had found what he had been looking for, for many years - peace.

I cannot forget the distress that one of my clients displayed when she first visited me a few years ago. Shona was a beautiful and very bright young lady, originally from Scotland, where she had trained as a speech therapist. At the time of the reading she was living and working in Greater Manchester. The reason for this distress was that her boyfriend, an oilrig worker, had come home on leave one weekend and had hung himself from the banister-rail of his parent's home. "What can I say to this person?" Were the words that filled my head, indeed what could anyone say to someone who has lost a friend or a relative in such tragic circumstances? I never said my job was easy! With this young man it was too soon for contact to be made, yet some very comforting spiritual words were given from a relative of Shona's, just to help her through this initial period of despair. Quite often relatives and friends of suicide victims feel they may be to blame in some way or even been the reason for their friend, or loved one, taking their own life. Her relative, in the Spirit world, then told Shona that she was not to blame. The reason was stress and financial difficulties, not a lot of comfort, but it did help a little on the day.

All of us will at some stage lose someone close, my mum once said to me, "as we get older we visit the graveyard more and more" that has certainly been true for me. I know I speak for most people when I say, there's nothing nice about physical death. Although, if the person who has died is elderly, or has died of an illness, it is difficult to accept, but easier to justify to oneself, than when a person chooses to end their own life. The views of society in general are that this is "an easy way out!" Or "surely they could have talked to someone about it!" "There are people to help!" Also, "nothing can be that bad!" Obviously it can and we have to except that, for some people, enough is enough and this is the right thing for them.

I wish, from the bottom of my heart, that my relatives who chose this path, could have resolved their problems or taken an alternative path. I realise that this is for myself and for the other relatives and friends that were left behind and maybe my selfish attitude. I want to close this chapter by saying I have had many spiritual contacts with people who have committed suicide, I draw my conclusion from the information that they have given to me. This being that the people who really wanted to die do so, they leave nothing to chance. When a person is only crying out for help, they will not take a large enough dose of tablets. They will make sure that they will be found in time before the tablets work. I remember the mother of a 21-year-old student coming to see me for a sitting. Her son had taken a massive drug overdose; the lady was desperate for me to tell her that her son had only done this as a cry for help. I couldn't do that, because her son made contact with me. He told me that his intentions were to die; he was under so much pressure from family and from life. Everyone was telling him what to do, what to study, how he should live his life and be successful. This he knew was for them, to please them or feed *their* egos. What he wanted didn't seem to matter to them. He told me he took the tablets early and went to bed, he was sure that he would not be disturbed, and he wasn't. His passing was very peaceful and took place in the middle of the night. He apologised to his mum for the shock and distress that finding his body had created, but he went on to say, "A body is better than no body". I did sense from this that the young man had thought about going missing; how or where I don't know. Being an intelligent, sensitive person he thought, at least this way there would be evidence of a physical ending.

To everyone out there who has experienced effects of a suicide death, please stop blaming yourself or carrying the guilt, unless in your heart you do have something to be guilty about. Respect the fact that this person made a choice, a very difficult choice. Help them and yourself by sending your love to them, and keep your heart and mind open to receive the love, which will be returned.

Remember - LOVE IS THE KEY.

Chapter Eight

Murder in a phone box.

This is the story of a young lady called Karen; she was brutally murdered in a telephone box a few years ago. So often we watch the national or local news and hear of terrible crimes such as murder. I must have been extremely naive in my past, because I believed that whenever someone was murdered it hit the headlines, either in the papers or on TV. Now I know this isn't so, I don't know how the media select the cases to publicise, but they are a small selection from many. Karen's murder did not receive publicity, but this did not make it insignificant in any way.

In 1995 I welcomed a lady into my home, she was a very quiet person, almost withdrawn. I like to pride myself that I can and do interact well with most people, both in my work and in my social life; however, this lady was the exception to the rule. I felt at first that I couldn't connect with her; everything I said just seemed to float above her head. She didn't talk to me or respond to my voice; still it's not in my nature to give up easily so I carried on.

I have learned from experience in doing my job, that when a person behaves in this manner they are waiting for something specific, a name of a loved one in Spirit or some specific information - I was right. Suddenly the atmosphere changed and the whole mood and tone of the reading altered.   I was then aware of a very strong female spiritual presence with us. The child, a grown-up child, had joined us. When I relayed these small details to my client, she raised her head, shuffled in her chair and instantly became more attentive. I looked at her face and it was as if a mask had been removed and we connected. "Thank God" I thought, I felt we were on our way to a really good sitting; I was right.

The connection with the Spirit became very strong "this is your daughter," I said. The lady's expression seemed to freeze with disbelief, mixed with relief as I spoke. Next I could feel a sensation in and around my throat, it got tighter and tighter, I felt as though I was struggling to breathe, at first very uncomfortable then painful. I was able to release myself from this intense feeling. I asked the lady if her daughter had been hung, "she was strangled" was the reply. Tears filled my eyes, even after many years of doing sittings I still get very emotional. I make no apology for this. In this particular sitting there were so many emotions reacting with each other, some coming from Karen, others I could feel from her mum, plus my own. I am only human! I just can't describe to anyone what it feels like when two souls are reunited through me, one on the earth plane and the other in the Spirit world. I attempt to do so by using the words magical and electric as well as overwhelming joy. I do know, regardless of the fact that this sort of contact is very draining for me, it is a privileged position to be in. I wonder if a midwife attending a home birth, an extremely private and intimate situation, feels like me. She, like me, is the outsider, yet she is vital to the situation.

A little time was used to establish that the Spirit really was Karen. Details were given and her mum was satisfied it was she. In the early part of the communication I had been working with feelings (clairsentience) then a soft voice spoke gently in my head, she wanted to tell her mum what had happened the night she was murdered. She knew her mum had been guessing and fantasizing about it, this would put an end to the speculation. I did ask my client if it was all right for me to continue, in other words, was she up to it? The answer was "yes". She told me it would be a relief to know. Karen told me she did know the man, but only for a short time - her mum confirmed this. She didn't say why she was in the phone box, only that the man turned nasty. He had put his hands around her throat; the pressure was so great that she passed out. He was so strong that he continued to squeeze even when her legs had collapsed beneath her; she was hanging from his hands (that's why I felt that she had hung rather than had been strangled).

I felt compelled to stop and apologise to my client for the unpleasant detail, she told me that it was better to know, Karen told me she passed very quickly, once she had passed out. She talked about the physical evidence conjuring up an image of great suffering, then she said "it was not what it seemed, "she was very frightened, that was the worst part, then there was pain, then there was nothing until she woke up in the Spirit world.

Karen relayed a lot of information to me using feelings. I was able to tell her mum she thought it was a blessing that the man had been so strong, because she had suffered less. Karen's mum told me it was a huge relief to know how Karen actually died. She felt she could come to terms with the grief, knowing the details; these had filled the gap.

What was lovely about this sitting was that Karen was such a chatterbox, just as I thought she had left us, she kept popping back with a few more words. She told me she was 19, she had celebrated her birthday just before she passed; this was correct. She brought a few very personal messages to mum, and then she seemed to fade into the background, throughout the rest of the sitting I was fully aware of her presence, she only departed when her mum left my house.

I just want to add that this murderer was caught and was given a very short sentence. I did this sitting in 1995, at that time Karen's mum told me the man would be released in about three years time 1998, which means that by now the man will be free.

Murder and crimes of extreme violence are on the increase. The cases we the public get to hear about are only the tip of the iceberg. Tragedy is all around us, whether it is a personal tragedy or national one, in the aftermath there are so many unanswered questions.

Physical death happens in many different ways, some of us go to sleep and never physically wake-up. For others it's a sudden transition such as a car crash or pain in the chest and they drop to the floor. There's something natural about these kinds of deaths, a shock, emotionally painful, but acceptable. Although we may not be present at the time of death we are provided with an image for our minds to work with, like working through a process from A to B. With a murder, or indeed a suicide, even though the body is found it doesn't end there.

The job of a good medium is to help the person or people left behind, sometimes there is no answer just detail, and this is like a gift to the grieving person. It gives them something to process in their minds, like building a bridge between themselves and the person who has gone on; suddenly the gap doesn't seem so wide. It can feel like a pathway on which they can emotionally travel in order to work through the grief process.

Having worked in various ways with bereaved people, I've discovered that some are afraid to work through their grief. If they do, they believe they will no longer feel the emotional pain. They will feel guilty, as though they will forget the person who has moved on in the Spirit world if they relinquish such feelings. One gentleman told me "if I'm not in pain then it means I'm not grieving for my wife anymore, which means I don't care about her". This is a surprisingly common belief; I have experienced it myself in the distant past.

The Spirits experience a period of grief just as we "earthlings" do. I feel their process is completed much quicker than ours is. I often get the feeling that they are patiently waiting for us to travel through this "dark tunnel" known as grief. Once we are out and back into the light we can reconnect, then they take hold of our hands and walk the way with us. The grief, "the dark tunnel", keeps us apart, that is why, apart from the initial period of time (2 or 3 days) after someone has passed to Spirit, there is often a lack of spiritual contact, we all need time to adjust, to relax and to heal. Apart from exceptional cases, I would never agree to do a sitting for someone recently bereaved, they would be disappointed, and for many it doesn't really help anyone, neither the bereaved nor the new Spirit, if they go for a sitting too soon.

Chapter Nine

A guest for tea.

In October 1996 I met a very gregarious young lady called Heather. Our meeting was purely social, before we met, she was aware of my background in mediumship so it wasn't long before the conversation moved around to the subject of spiritual matters. She asked me a question that I've been asked many times before; it was "what is it like when you see a ghost? "I answered with a very light-hearted question "do you mean is it like the character Jack in the film American werewolf in London?" "Yes" she replied. For anyone who hasn't seen the film, Jack was an American tourist on a walking holiday in England who was savaged by a werewolf on the moors. Throughout the film he appeared to his friend David to warn him that he was a werewolf, Jack's appearances were at various stages of decomposition.

Luckily I was able to convince Heather that wasn't normal it was just for the films. I have met a lot of people who've seen ghosts and not one of them has seen a mutilated or decomposed Spirit. To my knowledge the only mutilated Spirit I have heard of is that of Ann Boleyn, walking the bloody tower with her head tucked underneath her arm! Heather had had a special friend who had been run down by an army truck and killed. She so wanted to "see" him again but feared he would appear as a grotesque mess, I think not!

I have been very lucky, having experienced some spectacular, although at times unnerving, spiritual events and psychic activity. I have met a lot of people who have experienced far more than I have. I've been given accounts of amazing and extraordinary things. Some days I haven't been able to believe my luck when clients have shared their experiences with me.

These are very special accounts of spiritual experiences they are about the gentleman who came to tea, and about Joan. The reasons I've chosen these two examples are that they are very spiritual and emotionally intense, which had a profound effect on me as I hope they will have on you.

Before I begin to answer Heather's question "what's it like when you see a ghost?" They do appear in many forms. My favourite is in the form of a psychic light, a tiny spark of spiritual energy than either flashes or "dances" before you. I have seen a golden glow; this may be as small as a tennis ball or as big as a wall. Spirits can appear as a filmy, grey or white figure, they seem to float around leaving a lingering trail as they move on (the film Poltergeist has a scene, which demonstrates this classic ghostly figure). They often appear as a solid dark figure without features or texture, often caught out of the corner of ones eye; leaving us uncertain as to whether we have seen someone or was it a trick of the light?

We now move to semi-solid figures, with features often in colour and solid form, which sometimes can be touched, or more to the point, which can touch us! There is a state, where parts of the person are seen such as head and shoulders. In 1983 after the break-up of my first marriage I stayed with my aunt and uncle for a short time. They were both very open to spiritual things, the day after I left their home, my aunt was cooking in the kitchen when she looked out of the window and saw a pair of a "legs" walking towards the back door. She was so shocked she ran towards the back door and bolted it, and then she had to sit down with a glass of brandy. This story still makes me laugh, not the legs, but my aunt's actions. The legs never did appear inside the house but we don't think bolting the door would have stopped them entering had they wanted to!

I would like to say that Spirits often touch or kiss people, often without appearing at the same time. The story of Joan will give you a rare example of those things happening at the same time.

Firstly I want to tell you about a most interesting client her name was Mrs Massey. There were so many Spirit names at the start of her reading; I thought she had brought the whole Spirit world with her! Then the reading progressed and a name was given from the Spirit world, which triggered off a conversation that I shall remember all my life.

One afternoon, a few years prior to our conversation, she was at home alone. There was a knock on the door; she opened it to find a very familiar gentleman standing on the step. She hadn't seen him for a number of years, the reason for this being; he had "died".

As you can imagine, this was a lot to take in at first, however the story just got better. "What did you do?" I asked, she told me that she had invited him in, he was solid form, he looked marvellous, he looked younger than when she had last seen him in his earthly body, yet still very recognisable.

They sat down and he held her hand, they talked about everything that had happened since they had last seen each other, she did say there was a sense that he already seemed to know about the things she talked about. I asked her how this felt; she told me that, after the initial shock, it felt natural, as though he had never been away.

"What happened next?" I asked. Her father-in-law asked for a cup of tea so Mrs. Massey went into the kitchen to make it. When she returned to the sitting room with the tea, her father-in-law had gone. She was left standing with two cups of tea in her hand, which she placed on the coffee table; they remained there until her husband came home. When he entered the sitting room he said, "have you had visitors?" She answered, "Yes I have, your father".

I was spellbound when she gave me the account of this experience; then, I bombarded her with questions. "What did you think when you saw your father-in-law at your door?" She told me that at first she realised he was a Spirit. But that thought was gone in seconds. (It could have created anxiety, which would have stopped the flow of energy between them, which is necessary for any spiritual experience to occur) she didn't reason she just accepted his presence. I wanted to know what they talked about, "family and my health mainly", she said. When he was on this earth she had always loved and respected this man, so there was no element of fear or apprehension "it just felt right", she said.

I wanted to know what it felt like when he held her hand, (I've had an experience, which I should tell you about later, very different from this one) "it was lovely, and he felt very warm". She went on to describe a sense of comfort and reassurance mingled with some overwhelming joy. "It was wonderful, I shall remember it all my life". I had just one more question - what were her thoughts and reactions when she returned to the sitting room with the tea, to find him gone? She told me she felt very sad, then she started to shake with the shock, then she sat down and stared at the cups until her husband came home.

The experience I had with a Spirit holding my hand was very different. It happened in 1982. One morning I was awakened by a presence in my bedroom. My arm appeared to be reaching up high above my head, as I reached a high level of consciousness, I realised that this was not my doing. Someone had a firm grip on my hand. As soon as I realised this I started to try and pull my arm down, it was a struggle, at first the grip seemed to get tighter and tighter. Eventually I broke free and I put my hand under the covers faster than "greased lightning", followed by my head! My heart was thumping, it seemed to take ages to slow down and only when I had really composed myself did I emerge from the sheets. I told you at the start that I'm a bit of a coward. I didn't like this and I told the Spirits so, they haven't done it to me since.

When I really started to develop my mediumship, I frequently experienced a sensation that I can only describe to you as pins being stuck into my body. They wanted me to know they were there. I certainly got the message, so I told them to stop and they did. These days they are much gentler with me, they stroke my head or put their hands-on my neck or shoulders, it's lovely most of the time. I consider myself to be very lucky to have such experiences.

The story of Joan is also very special to me. Joan and I got acquainted when her husband came to see me about six months after her death. Once we had sat down and become at ease with each other, I commented on the sadness I could feel around him. I asked if he had suffered a great loss recently, to which he merely replied "yes", he didn't say anything else. It was only a short time until a female Spirit came very close to me and gave me the name Joan. The gentleman accepted the name so we went on. During the course of the sitting it was revealed that Joan was his wife, she had passed to Spirit after a long battle against cancer, leaving behind her husband and 12-year-old daughter.

When my work was completed and the gentleman was satisfied with the information given, he asked me if he could tell me about an experience he had recently had. I was more than willing to listen, as always, so he began. He hadn't slept well since Joan had passed over, but there had been one particularly bad night a few weeks previous to our meeting when he had been very restless, had had broken sleep. These are classic symptoms of someone that is worrying or grieving. Whilst he was having one of his calmer moments he felt a weight on the side of his bed, someone had sat down at the side of him. He opened his eyes and to his disbelief, then to his delight, he saw Joan sitting on the edge of the bed. She was looking at him and smiling, she spoke to him saying "hello". I asked him "how did she look?" "Very well" he replied. He told make she was naked from the waist upward, Joan died of breast cancer; she'd had a mastectomy, which unfortunately was done too late. She has suffered greatly before the end of her physical life. She appeared like this because she wanted John to see she was perfect again, something that had upset them both was the surgery. John told me she had never got over it or accepted it.

Joan took hold of John's hands and placed them on her body, then wrapped her arms around him and vice versa, the embrace seemed to last for hours but realistically it must have been for about 10 minutes. He told me she felt warm and soft, very very real, nothing was said verbally. They didn't need to talk. I asked very tentatively "what happened next"; he told me after a while she just started to fade away, as if she just dissolved into the night. He was left with his arms enfolding an area of thin air. He didn't see Joan go because his eyes were closed but he felt that was the best way, to see her leave would have been more difficult than feeling her go.

By the time he had finished his story, I was feeling extremely emotional, I thanked John from the bottom of my heart for being so generous and sharing this special experience with me. No matter how many people talk to me about their experiences, I never take any of it for granted. I'm still amazed and excited by the whole spiritual and psychic world. What I find really admirable is the way people are willing to take the risk and tell, knowing there are so many people out in the world ready to ridicule them. I predict for the future that there will be more and more people willing to open up and speak out about such matters. I think the world is ready to hear.

I want to continue the theme of Spirit visitors in solid forms. This time I will delve into my personal archive of spiritual experiences covering my family and me. I introduced you to my father, Henry, at the start of the book. To be more accurate, I introduced you to his beliefs, i.e. "when you're dead you're dead" etc. Those beliefs were shattered after my mum passed to Spirit in 1986. He took her "death" very hard indeed; this was the second time he had lost his wife. His first wife Jane "died" when she was 34, leaving three young children. Mum was 11 years his junior, I suppose, in his mind, he felt this was some sort of guarantee that she would out-live him and he would not be left behind to continue living alone, sadly he was disappointed. In fact, after she passed he told me "I didn't plan it this way".

Dad's health wasn't that good at the time of mum's "death" and from then on it took a downhill slide until his own passing two years later.

As a family we attended to dad in different ways, to the best of our abilities. Nothing could replace or compensate for the loss of mum, it was clear he was just existing, biding time until his loneliness came to an end. What we must remind ourselves of here is the fact that death meant the end through my dad's eyes.

About six months after mum's death on a Tuesday afternoon, 15th April, my sister made her daily visit to see him. She had no idea beforehand what kind of greeting she would receive on this day. She told me dad looked very pale, he stood in the middle of the room, he was so stressed he could hardly speak, for a few moments he just jiggled his feet about, his whole body look rigid, he just spewed out "I've seen your mam!" My sister was stuck for words, after all we had been brought up with this subject being a "no go" area. She just told him "I believe you" then changed the subject until I arrived a little later.

We went into the hall and she relayed the conversation to me. I joined dad and told him that I knew about mum's visit. At first he looked annoyed and embarrassed, then I started to ask questions which seemed to calm him. I guess he thought I would consider him to be "going strange". I asked him what mum was wearing, he answered "a pink night dress and a cardigan" I asked if she had spoken to him, "No" was the reply. "What happened?" I asked. He told us that he had woken very early, about 5.30 a.m. He opened his eyes and she was just there, standing at the bottom of the bed smiling at him, after a few minutes she "just went". I asked him if he had been scared, he told me "not at all", what I detected in his voice was an element of aggravation. I interpreted the feelings from his tone as a "Don't be stupid, there wasn't anything to be scared of". Very discretely my sister and I looked at each other, what ran through my mind was that I thought, "When you were dead you were dead!" very sarcastic I know, but I couldn't help it. He was a man who had gone to bed one night with a belief system concreted in place and within a few hours that whole system had been shattered into pieces. It was a lot for us to take in, what a turn around.

This visit was not an isolated event; there were numerous occasions during the next 18 months. What amused me was the fact that dad tried very hard to convince us that mum really had visited, which meant life really does go on after "death". He couldn't seem to grasp the fact that he was preaching to the converted! The visits did become more frequent and the duration lengthened. There were times when he was very open, giving every detail, but about others he was very secretive; they must have been special times.

Mum did appear in solid form on all occasions. Sometimes she spoke, but not always. Conversation must have been deeply personal; he was reluctant to share content. He always commented on how well she looked which, I feel, reassured him and gave him comfort. The pattern seemed to be the same; he would wake in the early hours and find her standing at the bottom of the bed or sitting in the armchair at the opposite side of the room.

Visits from a very close Spirit on a regular basis don't always mean that the person is going to pass to Spirit themselves, however, there is no doubt that for many it is part of the preparation. I have done readings for many nursing staff during my career, many of them have witnessed patients talking to what they can only presume is the Spirit of a loved one, shortly before their physical life ends. This is very commonplace, nothing unusual to us believers. A very reassuring thought for me personally, that at the end of my earthly life, there would be someone there to take my hand and lead the way.

Before closing this chapter, I must share with you a splendid spiritual experience that was told to me very recently by a client of mine, Margaret, who lives in Coventry. She is no stranger to psychic/spiritual happenings and often has experiences during the night. Her nightly ritual, around nine o'clock, is to take her little dog for a stroll up and down the road where she lives which is very quiet and almost always deserted at that time in the evening. One evening, whilst walking, she became aware of the smell of cigarette smoke wafting around her. She thought at first that someone may be following her, it made her a little anxious, so she looked around, saw nobody and made her way back home.

The next night the same happened and this continued for some weeks. Always being cautious she looked around but saw no one. Eventually she just accepted it, knowing that something was going on even if she didn't know what! Then, one evening things did change. Everything was as normal, a quiet evening, and then suddenly Margaret's dog started barking, in fact going "bananas!" Very unusual as he just loves people and is a normally placid animal. Margaret looked around to see what was upsetting him. There was a tall, slim man dressed in a raincoat tied at the waist. He was wearing a trilby hat and smoking a cigarette. He started a conversation about dogs telling her his was waiting for him at home, locked in the conservatory. Margaret was almost outside her door as their conversation came to a close. The man said "I'm the man who supplies your power during the night", then "Goodnight". This led her to think that the man worked for an electricity producing company. She turned as she approached her door to see which way he had gone. Much to her surprise he had vanished. She had only taken her eyes off him for seconds; there was nowhere he could have gone. She told me that at that point she realized she had just held a conversation with a ghost.

She soon concluded that the "power in the night" he talked about was the spiritual/psychic energy she needed for her various experiences. The nightly dog walking ritual continued but she has never seen "the man" since, nor has she smelled the smoke. This poses the question, how many people that we encounter each day are "earthlings"? How many are spiritual visitors? What do you think?

Chapter Ten

Criminal investigations.

My interest in the spiritual and psychic side of life goes back as far as I can remember, as I said before, I have always had a sense of "knowing" long before I understood anything about the subject. I grew up in a small urban town called Tyldesley about 10 miles from Manchester. In Leigh, a neighbouring town, there lived a lady called Helen Hill, a very well known and respected medium. I have spoken with lots of people who have had wonderful sittings from this lady and the general opinion was, that she was quite remarkable, and what a character!

Her work wasn't restricted to one-to-one sittings; from time to time she was approach by the police to assist with certain cases. A good friend of mind from way back, who had lived in Leigh all of her life, gave me details of a case that Helen had helped with. A man had disappeared from his home under very suspicious circumstances (I never found out the details). Mrs. Hill told the police that the man was dead; she described the place where his body could be found. The body was in the canal where it had got caught up on something in the water. After the police searched the place that Mrs. Hill had described they discovered the body. I was in my late teens when I heard this story and I recall being absolutely amazed by it. She instantly became one of my heroines, I felt that anyone with this marvellous gift deserved to be respected and admired.

I don't think for one minute that this case is a one off. It's just that we rarely get to hear about such matters, as it isn't the done thing! If the police, with all their experience and sophisticated equipment, can't solve a crime, then heaven forbid that they should stoop to "hocus-pocus"!

I often wonder what I would do if I "knew" some details that just might help solve a crime, the obvious answer is, go and tell. I do hesitate however, because in the Leigh area a few years ago, a young

girl called Lisa Hessian was murdered. At the time this case made regional news, so most people knew about it. Weeks after the murder; with the case still unsolved, a good friend of mine, Jim Walker, a very experienced medium in the Atherton area, had received some clairvoyant pictures which he believed were connected to this case, and which he felt could be helpful to the police. Being a dutiful citizen he didn't hesitate, off he went to the police station. Firstly he spoke to the officer on the front desk, and was asked to wait. When this officer had spoken to a senior officer, he returned and asked Jim if he would mind accompanying him to an interview room. Jim didn't mind he wanted to help all he could. However, the situation did a U-turn, suddenly it was Jim who was in hot seat. The details that he gave about the scene of crime were very accurate, the policeman seemed to think that anyone who knew so much must have been involved or linked to the person who committed the crime. So this good deed backfired.

Eventually Jim convinced the police that he was not involved, he was treated like a crank and sent off with an unspoken message, but a very strong feeling of "go away and forget it". When Jim told me about this we managed to laugh it off, even though he was angry and frustrated at being dismissed, he felt that he could have helped, had they taken the trouble to really listen. "I'll never offer again," he said to me and I don't believe he has to this day.

I can appreciate the "guts" it takes for any medium or psychic to come forward with information to any person in authority. Back in 1997 there were a series of IRA bombs and bomb scares, at times great areas of the county have been brought to a standstill. The Midlands area was the biggest to be effected. On the Sunday before this happened, I got up to make a cup of tea, it was about eight o'clock, I experienced the weirdest psychic feelings. I felt I was in Telford town centre and had to run into a toilet for shelter because there was a bomb alert. It was a very intense feeling, so I told my husband, Martin. Within the week there was a massive bombs scare, I know it didn't happen in Telford centre, but I realised immediately that I had been given something I could relate to, in order that I should take notice, and that Telford centre wasn't really relevant. But I did wonder what to do about it, and decided in the end to do nothing. A week or so later I had a similar experience. I felt I was driving across Tower Bridge in London, I felt panic, I knew the IRA was near. A few days later I heard on the radio that London had been brought to a virtual standstill by bomb scares, as were two airports. I wonder what you would do with "knowings" like this?

Regardless of the fact that I haven't helped the police with one of their criminal investigations, doesn't mean to say that I haven't had any experience in that field of work. My ex-husband worked for some time for a small firm of accountants owned by Keith. He ran this small easy-going concern with a very laid-back style; he was a very trusting sort of person. It was an enormous shock to him when he discovered he was employing a criminal. I won't name the person involved, but I can tell you that the nature of this man's crime was very serious and could have had a profoundly destructive effect on Keith's firm if the man had not been exposed when he was.

I was alerted to the situation purely by chance. Tyldesley has a carnival once a year, so I decided to take full advantage and view the parade from an elevated position, the upstairs front office of my ex-husband's workplace. I looked out of the window thinking "the best view in town". I didn't want to stand for the whole thing however, so I took a seat in the nearby chair. A very comfortable chair, it had a high back and it swivelled around. I leaned back and felt compelled to close my eyes, I started to feel very strange indeed, as though someone had "switched me on" the mode I am in when I do a sitting, yet in this case it was involuntary.

It took me a few moments to realise what was happening "I was on duty" so to speak. Then the most dreadful feelings of deceit, lies and fraud came over me. This chair belonged to the man whose office I was in, a man "who would steal the pennies from a dead man's eyes" that wasn't a term I would use personally, so I realised very quickly that I was being given some very serious information. What on earth should I do with it - to tell or not tell? I moved out of the chair and the feeling stopped immediately, which didn't mean I could forget or dismiss what I knew. Just to be sure I sat in the chair again, all the feelings flooded back. I decided to think about it for a few days, but the burden of carrying this information was too heavy. These were serious accusations and what if I was wrong? What if I had imagined it all? I had to have faith in myself, I mentally examined my track record, and I knew my information had proved to be reliable to so many clients in the past, why should this be any different? I passed the information on to Keith.

Thankfully for me the information was treated with great regard, although at that point, none of us knew exactly what we were dealing with or where it might lead: I said that I felt the desk had the answers. This threw out another major dilemma, but not for me this time. Keith had to decide whether or not to open the desk that was locked, invading another person's privacy is not a pleasant thing to do, especially if it leads to nothing, but Keith knew it was very very necessary.

A few days later the desk was opened and the truth was discovered. This man had been using other people's money to make money. Using their money to make personal investments without permission. Many of these deals had failed so, he made even more deals, in the hope that he could right the wrong he had already done. There was so much documentary evidence in the drawer that it was clear to see that this man had dug a hole for himself, so big and deep that it had become impossible to climb out.

His personal clients had already discovered some of his fraudulent actions. Amongst his papers were documents from the courts. These gave dates for his hearings, and of the pending bankruptcy hearing. What a mess this man had got himself into. It was obvious that the reason I was alerted to the situation was in protection of Keith. It was, and probably still is, illegal for a firm of accountants to employ a bankrupt.

For a long time after the event, I wondered whether it would have been better to keep quiet. Then I reasoned this out by saying, "we are only given information that is useful and will serve a positive purpose" otherwise it is just spiritual gossip. The man did get a prison sentence for his offences; maybe being discovered saved him from himself in the long run.

The headline in the local paper that followed the court case read "swindling accountant jailed" and I told myself that, even if I hadn't intervened in the situation, the whole thing would have blown up eventually, but by speaking out, it alerted Keith. He was able to dismiss the man, before the court case, which did save him a lot of embarrassment and probably a lot of money and clients in the long run.

I was very flattered when I was asked to give advice with regard to the aftermath of this event. I did this by holding papers and documents that were found in the desk and which belonged to some of Keith's clients (psychometry). A variety of details were discovered. I passed them on to Keith, who was then alerted to those clients who had been affected, and he was able to approach them before they realised anything was wrong, this probably saved his business.

There are, to my knowledge, a number of mediums in the country that do "psychic detective" work, it must be very demanding. I found my experience very intense and stressful, I know Keith was helped, but I can honestly say I didn't really get any satisfaction from the experience. I felt "charged up" and on a sort of "high", but not a pleasant sort of high. I then said to myself that if anyone were to approach me for help of this nature in future, I would do my best, but would never go out of my way to look for it. That was in 1989 and thankfully this sort of case hasn't come my way yet!

Chapter Eleven

Visual Phenomena

Even though I don't do any face-to-face work at the time of writing, I write from having a wealth of experience of doing so. On days that I was feeling particularly anxious, more often than not my feelings matched those of my client. I felt that it was my job to put my client at ease as quickly as possible so that work could begin.

Newcomers to this business of having sittings would often ask me questions right from the start. Probably the most common one being "will anything happen?" Or "will I see anything?" My usual answer would be, "If anything happens I will be the first one out of here!" this would usually get a laugh and put the person at ease. Spirits are very gentle with us in general, the last thing they would want to do, would be to frighten us away by doing some kind of "party trick". They do treat us accordingly, not only in the way they decide to produce something visual or not, but in the way to give me the messages or information. Some of us can take it on the nose, some of us can't. People shouldn't be put off having sittings; we are all individuals and will be treated that way.

I must have done thousands of sittings over the years; most have been completed without any spiritual/psychic activities taking place outside myself. However, there have been a considerable number where minor to major psychic or spiritual happenings have proved to be the highlight of the session. The most common experience has been the client seeing psychic lights, flashing off the wall or sometimes hovering about my person. These are so beautiful; they are either extremely colourful, like a jewel or piercingly bright like a diamond. One client interrupted me by shouting; "Did you see that?" I asked what she had seen because I hadn't. "That flash on the wall", the lady was so excited, it was her very first experience of this kind.

More often than not I was the one lucky enough to see the lights, I could never continue the sitting without commenting, telling them something like "there's a beautiful light dancing by the side of you" or wherever. I think clients have a right to know what is happening around them, after all this is their time and space. People have been quick enough to tell me when they have either seen or felt something during the sitting. A very common experience, which has often being shared with me is, a drastic change in room temperature. We have shivered in the heat of summer, and experience hot flushes in the depths of winter. No joke, I can tell you, with the latter I have often had to remove a layer of clothing, then within a few minutes put it back on again. They do this to make us fully aware of their presence, a voice or a clairvoyant picture will achieve that but some Spirits must feel they have to reach drastic measures in order for us to take notice of them.

I have been rummaging through my mental archive, and have decided on four outstanding examples of visual experiences during my sittings. The first one takes me back to the early days of my career. An elderly lady called Lilly came to see me, what a character; she was well into her 70s and still bursting with enthusiasm for life. This was one of those days when I could hardly get a word in, nevertheless the sitting went well, the atmosphere was well charged and the messages flowed. Suddenly she said "stop, stop" she pointed her finger at me and said "I have to tell you what I can see, there is a man at the side of you". She had a look of shock on her face, but I must admit that I was the one who was really shocked. The hairs on my arms and neck just stood up. I asked her to tell me more, which she did, "I can just see his head and he's smiling". She went on to describe his features, I recognised them as my grandfather's, my mum's father, James Henry, and I have told you about him earlier. Even though he passed to Spirit before I was born, I recognised him from photographs that my mum had. I had mixed feelings with this, as well as feeling quite emotional. Never before had anything like this happened in a sitting, one minute I was the medium, the next, we had changed roles. I will admit it disrupted me quite a lot. I was very glad that the sitting was almost complete, when my granddad decided to show himself, it was difficult to carry on after that, but I did and Lilly was well satisfied.

Lilly and I had a chat after the sitting. She had been seeing Spirits since she was a child, no voices or sensations, no messages or predictions. I told her she had a wonderful gift and that I knew a number of professional mediums that would give their right arm to have her gift. Most mediums that "see" do so clairvoyantly not objectively. Lilly didn't recognise this as a gift, to her it was a way of life "they are everywhere" she told me.

One of my more relaxed clients is Karen, a regular visitor to me over the years. Having a sitting with me was one of her "treats". I'm quite a modest person, probably due to my upbringing, however, I have learned to accept a genuine complement and take it on-board. This was a sign that what I was doing was valued by others and extremely worthwhile. When a client feels relaxed and comfortable with me, the energy just seems to flow from them to me, to the Spirits and vice versa, this really makes the work a lot easier.

The last sitting Karen had with me was different from normal to say the least. I was doing my "stuff" then I realised that Karen had become very distracted. I watched her eyes, they were drawn to my half glass kitchen door, her face changed, she became quite pale, then she said "there's a man in your kitchen", "A man, what kind of a man?" I replied knowingly. The back door was locked, so I knew that no human being could be in there. Karen said, "He's tall and slim, wearing a dark coat and a hat". I didn't recognise him as one of "mine", so I asked her if seeing Spirits was a normal occurrence for her. "No, definitely not" she replied, "I've never seen one in my life" to which I laughed and said "you just have". When we investigated further we discovered he was "one of hers". As she was leaving the house I said, with tongue in cheek, "would you mind taking him with you, because I've got enough of my own!" She looked at me in a way that would suggest mixed feelings. Half smiling half frowning - she told me she was still in shock, she was glad she had had this experience but on the other hand she was spooked! She didn't like the thought of taking him with her, my hopefully reassuring reply was "once you get over the shock you will feel quite privileged", and I hope I was right.

On two occasions I've been lucky enough to share a visual experience with my client. Almost always it is the client or me that witnesses the spectacle. Susan was a lady I have known for many years and I recently found out that she now is herself in the Spirit world. She was no stranger to tragedy and trauma, her life read like a catalogue of sad events. The sitting I want to tell you about took place on a winter's evening. Everything was going so well, the spiritual contact was very strong, Susan was an excellent client, by that I mean that she was so relaxed with the spiritual side of life, she acted as a sort of conductor. It felt as though she was supplying the energy for the sitting to take place rather than me. I used to wish there were more people like her, to make life easier for me!

We reached a point in the sitting when both our eyes were drawn to the end of the table. A stream of light appeared measuring about two feet tall, the best way I can describe it to you is as being similar to one of those lava lamps that were so popular in the '60s. A tube of coloured liquid with glitter and bubbles floating around inside when the light was switched on. The stream of light we saw was a fluorescent glow, there was something sparkly moving around within the light, then a small white feathery object floated down very slowly, it reached the table, then it was gone.

This was magical, the experience lasted about 10 seconds, it doesn't sound a lot but it was. We looked at each other and said, "Did you see that?" Yes we did and we couldn't believe our eyes. I think it must be one of the nicest spiritual experiences I have had, there was a feeling of peace and calm in my dining room, time felt as though it had stood still for those seconds.

I didn't understand at the time of the sitting what the relevance of it was. It didn't connect in any way to the subject matter of the sitting. In retrospect I can now understand it, or least why it happened to Susan; during the years that lay ahead her pathway was studded with sadness and trauma. Already a firm believer in the Spirit world, this was a bonus, something that would hopefully give her comfort and strength as she worked through the bad times that lay ahead, especially if her faith wavered, as it does sometimes for most of us when we are being tested. Her son committed suicide at a very early age and her daughter in law "died" very suddenly of a brain tumour whilst only in her mid 20s (There's a whole chapter about Lisa later in the book).

As human beings there are only so many knocks we can take, our faith and beliefs do take a battering, they might even get crushed. Being able to look back on a spiritual experience like this one, can help revive those beliefs and restore the faith that is needed to lift us out of the "pit" that grief and emotional pain can push us into.

At this stage I want to introduce you to Loraine, firstly as my client, then as a very interesting person in her own right. On first meeting I soon discovered Loraine to be a very spiritual and ultra sensitive person, to say a complicated person would be an understatement. We discussed work, her personal life that was in turmoil and her psychic and spiritual development. Somehow I felt a little out of my depth; however, I have tried never to back off from a challenge so I ploughed on. I seemed to go round and around in circles, my eyes were closed, I was trying to work with the information I was given without any visual distractions. What a shock I had when I opened my eyes, for the first time in my life I was witnessing a transfiguration. This means the image of a Spirit appears on or in front of the person, almost like placing a mask in front of the face, sometimes the two, the face and the spiritual image, seem to merge together. I was scared, I felt paralysed with fear, after a few moments I said sharply "I don't like this!" in an instant Loraine's face returned to normal, I was flushed and my heart was pounding in my chest. I just wanted her to leave. As I write this today I feel very embarrassed about my reaction and how I handled the situation, what I didn't value at the time was that I was witnessing a kind of miracle and I didn't realise. I can only put that down to my lack of experience, I do wonder what might have developed if I had handled the situation better.

That experience took place in 1984; Loraine and I are still in contact even though I now live in another part of the country (Shropshire). I witnessed just one of many such transfigurations that took place around that time. In front of me is a letter, which I received from Lorraine, it describes in detail another occasion when her "Spirit guide" made an appearance, and this was in a totally different circumstances. I hope you enjoy the account I am sure you will find it very interesting.

"Into the 1980s I was going through a very stressful time in my personal life and at work. Gradually over about three months I started to feel I was not alone, as if there was a much stronger person inside my body and mind. I was aware of this feeling in situations when I was upset or tearful". (Loraine was upset when I did the sitting for her and the Spirit guide began to materialise) "I became aware also that I started to feel that I couldn't go on in this life, the power of whatever was inside me seemed to get stronger and more angry"

Loraine goes on to describe how a pattern was beginning to form whenever she was upset she started to feel as though she was going to burst out of her skin. Soon she realised that the Spirit guide was doing this to protect her, because her health was suffering through stress. Keeping calm was the key - easier said than done, but it was easier to keep calm than to allow her Spirit guide to create these unpleasant feeling. She affectionately calls her Spirit guide "Mr. Angry".

The experience she tells me about happened a few weeks after the transfiguration that I had witnessed. Lorraine was at work, (she was a supervisor in a clothing factory) there was a confrontation with a YTS girl called Susan, "Mr. Angry" went further than he had done before. This is what she tells me.

"Susan was sent to my department to help out, I had had Susan training with me previously and she was a very keen worker, just what I needed that morning. Susan had other ideas, she said she didn't feel like doing any work and just wanted to talk. She wanted my advice on her boyfriend, job, hairstyle and anything she could think of. I always enjoyed our chats together, but that morning I just didn't have the time and I told her, once our work was complete for the day we could have our usual advice chat. As the morning went on I was getting very annoyed with her, so much so that I felt that if I didn't give her a slap (which is not in my nature normally) I would burst into tears, she was getting me so annoyed. Finally I went to the rest room for a five-minute rest to cool down. In she came, she started saying she wasn't going to be my friend anymore and asking why didn't I like her anymore.

Within seconds I felt I was rapidly growing in size, I felt as if my skin was about to burst open. I was trying to keep calm but I knew this time the situation was taken out of my hands. Next I felt my face; it seemed to shatter like a pane of glass, and it felt like another face was breaking through. I never took my eyes off Susan, I could hear her shouting, "please stop, don't, please stop I'm sorry" at this point she ran out of the room."

Loraine took a few minutes to come down and then went to find Susan; she goes on to say, "Before she would tell me what had happened, what she had seen, I had to promise never to do it again. (Do what? I didn't know what happened.) It took a while for her to calm down. She then told me what she had seen, a solid body grew out of my body, no clothes except for something wrapped around his waist, he looked like a native American Indian. She told me what had made her hysterical was, not only seeing the figure appear, but the power she felt being directed at her from the figure."

Susan and Lorraine remained friends for the time that they continued to work together. Lorraine tells me "Mr. Angry" hasn't revealed himself for many years, however, she knows he still exists, he is her protector, I know he exists because I saw of glimpse of him.

Lorraine has a spiritual gift that she has used to help others from time to time. We all have a niche in life or within a job or profession. My opinion is that Loraine shouldn't work with people on a one-to-one basis, she should develop her gift to a higher level, and I feel that when "Mr angry" appeared to Susan, The Spirit guide used ectoplasm as a medium to manifest himself. This makes Loraine capable of physical mediumship. I also feel she could become an excellent transfiguration medium. There are only a few of either in this country, having been lucky enough in 1982 to attend the séance when physical mediumship was witnessed, I can only comment by saying it was sensational.

Chapter Twelve

Humour from the Spirit world.

The job of a medium doesn't mean that I only have to deal with people who are upset or grieving. If life is going well, then there's no need to consult anyone for help, not just a medium, a doctor or lawyer. It is in times of trouble or distress that we turn to professionals for help. People have said to me in the past "I don't know how you cope with all these unhappy people" or "does it get you down?" Firstly, no, the job doesn't get me down, just because I deal with other people's problems, doesn't mean I take them on board and live with them. Also, what many people don't understand is that, physical death and grief is only a small part of what I deal with in my work. If I had to say I had a speciality it would be, "futures", showing people what lies ahead on their path, offering advice and guidance on the information given by the Spirits or at a psychic level. Where the bereaved are concerned I don't actually deal with that many.

I feel quite strongly that people may have a sitting too soon after a passing; everyone needs time to adjust, then to recover from the shock. A time to heal is needed before we are ready to make contact with the person that "is lost", also, the person who is in the Spirit world needs time to heal and adjust. I always feel there's a right time to re-unite and if we listen to our inner voice it will tell us when. Please give yourself some time to recover, unless you are a "veteran sitter" very used to having sittings, and you need to consult a medium about issues surrounding the "death" or deceased.

One thing I learned from doing my Job is that people don't change, personality wise, the moment they enter the Spirit world. If they were jovial on the earth, then this is relayed in the messages they give. On the other hand, if they were cantankerous or critical, be sure that will come through also. I must be fair to a lot of Spirits; they do seem to mellow; however, for some, this process can take months, even years. There are certain Spirits who remain bitter and angry for a very long time after their transition to Spirit. Most Spirits transmit love, warmth and affection and a vital part of my job is to pass that love on to my clients I liken it to passing on a gift from the Spirits.

I feel that to possess a sense of Humour is vital to life, but I do realise that not everyone would agree with me. What is a good sense of humour? We all perceive Humour in different ways and the Spirits are no different, I would like to demonstrate with a few examples.

Brenda came to see me after her husband Bill had been in the Spirit world about the year. She had dealt with the initial stages of grieving and came to me because she was very troubled. Immediately the sitting began I linked into this feeling, I told her what I felt and she agreed with me. At that moment Bill joined us, a strong powerful character that didn't mince his words. He told me his name, and then he told me "I went out like a light". This man had no problem communicating with me his words were loud and strong, almost a "matter of fact" attitude and I heard a snap of fingers. Next there was a moments silence which Bill broke with a loud laugh, "tell her that's how it was, it worries her that I suffered at the end" I gave Brenda the messages, which were accompanied by a clairvoyant picture of a light bulb shattering into minute pieces. I felt the message and its tone was quite cold. I didn't really like passing it on to Brenda. I need not have feared as she was so relieved she said "thank God for that" and got up from the chair came over to me and kissed me on the cheek. I'm sure that if I had given her £1000 she wouldn't have been happier. I wasn't sure what I had done to deserve this, but she went on to tell me that after Bill's passing, her imagination had been running riot, conjuring up all sorts of images of how he died. She was not with him when he suffered his fatal heart attack, her mind had created the worst scenario possible, of him fighting for life and suffering horrendous pain, and this message had in fact laid a ghost in Brenda's mind.

She told me she would be able to sleep now and that she didn't consider the tone of the message as being cold. From this she recognised Bill, it's how he was when he was on the earth. Straight and to the point with an almost wicked sense of humour which not many people appreciated. He had been the king of the "one liners" he would also wind people up and they never knew if he was joking or not. Brenda recognised him from his style, had he come through with a loving, gushy message, then that would have meant nothing to her.

The sense of humour that my next Spirit displayed, to me, was almost disturbing but his partner recognised it as part of his nature. Sandra came to see me for a reading because her relationship with her partner Phil had ended very abruptly. The sitting started very well, I was establishing a working relationship with Sandra, when I became aware of another presence, that of a male Spirit in the room. At first he didn't have anything to say for himself, but I was able to describe his character to my client. She nodded with acceptance of the details, it was clear to me that she recognised the man immediately. Then, I felt a sort of jolt, which shook my whole body, and then there was a bright red flash in my head. This was a first for me, just when you think you've seen or felt everything in this work something new pops up and surprises you! I relayed what I was experiencing to Sandra, there was also a feeling of great confusion within me, I could see and feel, but I couldn't understand. She said she understood, "that's typical of him, he would find it funny". I had to ask, "who would find what funny?" to which she replied, "A crate fell off a fork-lift truck at work and crushed him, it was like something out of a slap-stick comedy film. If Phil could have chosen a way to die, this would have been it, no suffering, over in a second" and that's exactly how this man "died", in an instant. Sandra said she was comforted by the message and she said that the way he had communicated convinced her that it was him and that he hadn't changed.

For most of us, the development of mediumship is very difficult. It's a lonely time and it seems that there's no one to turn to, no one who understands. I was incredibly lucky to have had the help and support of a medium called Stephen Kirk; he was my mentor in the early days. He taught me a very important lesson, "whatever you get you must give, and no matter how trivial or nonsensical it may seem to you at the time". I soon learned to do as Stephen had told me but some of the results were annoying.

Here are a couple of examples, which not only demonstrate how an obscure message can have such a lot of meaning for the client, but that the Spirit's sense of humour is integrated in the message. I wonder if most of you are familiar with the nursery rhyme "four and twenty blackbirds baked in a pie". These words were given to me as a message from the Spirits to my client. As I repeated them to my client, I was suddenly aware that I was trying to suppress laughter; I did this because I felt it rude to make light of any message from the Spirit world. It would have been very different if the message had been overtly funny. The Spirit identified herself as my client's grandmother; she was a lovely, jolly character. The moment I quoted the rhyme, my client broke into an enormous grin that progressed to laughter "I fully understand" she said, then she proceeded to tell me a story. "Once I went to my gran's for tea, a wonderful cook, she had baked a number of pies that day, one of which was an apple pie which she was serving for sweet with custard. As she cut open the pie, she was quite horrified to discover it was meat! Immediately she burst into song *four and twenty blackbirds baked in a pie*".

My client went on to say that this had made her day, there was no doubt in her mind that the contact was her Gran. The pie incident had occurred when she was a child and had never been forgotten by anyone, it was a valuable member of the family's collection of funny stores. It was all the evidence she ever needed of her Gran's survival.

Details from another sitting which may amuse you took place at the end of 1994. This lady was a new client to me, but not new to spiritualism or having sittings. We were in immediate rapport, the messages and information just flowed so easily, and the atmosphere was highly charged and filled with positive feelings. A lovely Spirit joined us. I could not see him in my mind, I sensed him close by, a strong and loving personality. I could feel him as being a tall person, well built, his warmth and character were overwhelming, and there was also a fatherly feeling with him.

The lady said "yes that's my dad, you're describing him to a tee". There were a number of personal messages to pass on, some of which were very emotional, both my client and I had tears running down our faces, the love just flowed so easily between all three of us. Then I was compelled to stand up; I put my hands on my hips and swivelled the top of my body from side to side. The Spirit gentleman asked me to say to his daughter "what do you think of my new figure?" I must say I felt silly standing there with my hands on my hips swirling around like a little girl showing off her new party frock! He told me to tell her he now had a 32 in. waist. I did manage to sit down and she explained that her dad had had a 54 in. waist before he passed to Spirit. He had been very unhappy with himself for a long time, apart from the obvious discomfort; his health had suffered due to him being so overweight. Not long before he "died" he put himself on a diet, which mainly consisted of crab apples and more crab apples, at this point I heard his voice in my ear, he said "I was bloody sick of crab apples!" We laughed a lot during the sitting, my client told me the messages had meant a lot to her, knowing her dad was happy with himself made all the difference to her. She told me he was always laughing; he seemed to make everyone smile. He certainly had that effect on us that day. The truth seems to be that whatever our personality comprises, we take into Spirit, happy and jovial souls, remain that way. If we were "old misery guts" that won't change overnight, all this is worth thinking about. Time for self-assessment maybe, is how we are, how we want to be forever?

Chapter Thirteen

"What doesn't feel like to die?"

One thing and only one thing is guaranteed in life and that is that one day we will all "die". It isn't healthy for any of us to dwell on the circumstances of our own physical decline, but when that time arrives I do hope that God will be merciful and my passing will be peaceful!

This sounds very silly but dead bodies; coffins and undertakers still give me the "willies". I have felt like this since I was a child. I'm aware that I do, and have always joked about these subjects; it is an obvious effort to counter my fears. When my cousin Brian decided to become an undertaker at the age of 16, I couldn't believe it. One-day whilst he was in the very early stages of his training, he handed me a book, it had a black cover and was clearly well used "this is a good

read," he said as he pushed it into my hand "it's an embalming handbook". I can tell you I felt quite faint. I remember thinking; "this is all we need, to have our very own family undertaker". Years later when I started working as a medium it really made me smile, I joked with Brian on various occasions "you deal with them at this end and I'll deal with them at the other end". My profession made him feel as creepy as his did me.

People tell me that as we get older and nearer to physical death, the whole thing doesn't scare us as much. For many people it does not scare them at all. I seem to have been surrounded all my life with elderly people, so I have a large number of statements on which to base these findings. For most people there has been a time in their lives when they have mentally confronted the issue of their own death and the reactions are varied from a shudder, to instant dismissal. "I can't bear to think about it" or "I'll deal with that when the time comes" attitude.

To know how someone felt physically, mentally and emotionally at the time of their passing can be a great comfort to the people left behind, as we demonstrated earlier in the book, the gentleman who "went out like a light" and Karen in the phone-box. Obviously I can only speak about the Spirits that I have had communication with, which I do believe is a good cross-section of the Spirit world community. They tell me the transition is almost instant, (my translation of this is, it does take time, but time as we know it is not Spirit time - instant to them could be hours to us). Most tell me "one minute you are on the earth with earthly feelings such as pain, distress, regret or even loneliness and they just stop the moment we awaken in Spirit, or recognise we are there". It is very difficult to imagine what that must be like. I'm writing this chapter on a very hot August afternoon, in the grounds of Stokesay Castle in Shropshire. It is so peaceful here; everything feels as near perfect in life at this moment as we could wish for. I wonder if the Spirit world is anything like this? There would be the added bonus of friends and family that have gone on before me - If this is heaven, there's nothing to fear!

Spirits often make themselves known during a sitting by bringing details, which were relevant at their time of death, physical details or symptoms of an illness are given. One man, who died in a car crash, gave me the sensation of broken windscreen piercing my face, I have "felt" a number of broken necks and heart attacks. Yes, it is a bit morbid. I believe we all have a sprinkling of morbid curiosity in our souls. In spiritual work it would seem a certain amount of "gory" detail must be relayed to the client in order to convince them that their loved one lives on. It also gives a kind of permission for the clients to get on with living their lives.

The people who "awake" in the Spirit world are those who have passed over after being in a coma or in a sleep-state. They seem not to remember anything at all about the transition; they simply "wake up" on the other side. They must feel a little bemused or confused. I guess it's like going to bed one evening in familiar surroundings, then waking up the next morning in some foreign land. The main difference being in a foreign land you would be surrounded with strangers who would speak in a foreign tongue, as opposed to old familiar faces speaking the same language as you. They tell me it is still a great shock and there is the feeling of grief for the people who have had to be left behind. The grief however, is different; it is a mental procedure not an emotional one.

There are some Spirits who do remember "the journey" but in my experience, not many. I have gathered more detail from people I have met that have had "near death experiences". Some people get halfway there, others have set foot in the Spirit world, they were still connected by a "silver chord", a spiritual umbilical cord that prevents us from becoming resident in the spiritual world as long as one end is connected to the earth plane. Many of these people have very vivid details of their journey, who and what they saw whilst making it. They tend to express a great sadness of having to return to the earth plane. I feel anyone who is sceptical but willing to listen would learn and understand a lot more through having a conversation with a person who had had a near death experience than by having a sitting with a medium. I have never considered that my mission in life is to convince anyone or change their beliefs; it has always been to help people to deal with this business of living.

During my career I have "felt" all kinds of deaths. The Spirits have spared me nothing and I sometimes feel they have taken great delight in it!! I guess many of them have a weird sense of humour. Here is an assortment of examples, so that you will understand what I mean. A very "kind" Spirit called John almost knocked me off my chair one day as I was doing a sitting. He gave me a pain, the pain he had felt the second before he had "died". It felt like an iron bolt shooting through my left shoulder and diagonally across my chest. I remember shouting out "bloody hell, who have we got here" John was my first heart attack victim from the Spirit world, he had one of those weird senses of humour, he allowed the feeling of pain to linger longer with me than he needed. It really took my breath away for a moment and I got extremely shirty with him, I said out loud "stop it now, we've got the message" he did, but very reluctantly.

From a spiritual point of view I have experienced a lot of heart attacks, even though it's usually very quick, it's extremely painful. I would advise anyone to look after his or her heart, I certainly try to, and dying of a heart attack is not the best way to go even though it is usually very quick!!

Death for many people is a lovely experience (they - the Spirits, tell me so). Some people die in their sleep, which is described to me as a dreamy, floating sensation, a feeling of drifting. This applies to people who in many cases have fought an illness for a long period of time. The time comes at the end of their physical life when they are taking drugs to keep them pain-free - It's such a blessing from a spiritual point of view, the body and mind may be drugged, but the Spirit is not affected. The body and mind stop fighting, and the Spirit is set free. One lady who had suffered with cancer told me "what a lovely way to go". I must also say that this is only successful if the person feels mentally at peace and is ready to pass.

Let's look at suicide from this angle, how does it feel? This may all sound a little flippant or light-hearted considering we are discussing such an emotive subject. What you have to remember is that I am quoting our Spirit friends. One such Spirit who hanged himself told me "Hanging is not good!" he went into some detail which could be hurtful or offensive to anyone who has lost a person this way. The point I want to share is that "there was no pain, just a moment of panic; then peace".

Pamela came for a sitting on a very dark dismal afternoon just before Christmas a few years ago. She was a long-standing client, who seemed to have the properties of a magnet where troubles and problems were concerned. She seems to carry the weight of the world on her shoulders. Having always tried my best to help her I often felt inadequate. Looking back on the work I had done for Pamela over the years and making my statement from feedback she gave me, inadequate was how I felt at the time not how I actually was. So much of the spiritual work I did helped and reassured her into the future. It feels like that with some clients; I just felt that, where she was concerned, I was the wrong person for the job.

This sitting was a particularly difficult or heavy one to do. Right in the middle of it I started to feel very uncomfortable, especially my chest, no pain just a weighty feeling. I ignored the feeling at first; then, the more I ignored it, the stronger it got. Breathing became more difficult and I had to say what I was feeling. At first Pamela looked puzzled, it was clear she couldn't understand. Then I had the voice of a young man in my ear, he told me he had passed over suddenly and he gave me his name. I was able to pass these small details on to the lady along with a description of feeling as though I had a slab of concrete on my chest; I couldn't feel pain, just the weight.

I wasn't familiar with these feelings; I wasn't given any more details verbally from the Spirit so I felt confused about the whole thing - a bit useless really. (Sometimes it's like that, feelings and emotions are given all at once but very little verbal detail, the whole experience becomes impossible to unravel. It's at times like this that I depend on my client to help me). Pamela was more than keen to help. She knew the name of the Spirit; he was a friend of her son's who had very recently killed himself. He had attached a hose to the exhaust pipe of his car, which he had parked on the canal bank, and filled the car with fumes.

Straight away the feelings left me "thank God for that!" I said. This was a lovely soul; he had been in his early '20s when he decided he couldn't face life anymore. He had come through to Pamela so that she could tell her son and his other friends that he was all right. People had been very upset at the way he had died; he wanted them all to know that the only sensation he had experienced was that of a weight on his chest as he fell asleep.

As a medium I'm always learning that there is always a surprise or a challenge in readings. That day, I had to rely on help, but the next time this sensation was given to me, I recognised it and knew exactly how my client had passed over, it certainly cut down on the "suffering" for me!

One Sunday during the summer of 1995 my friend Dawn came to visit me, we had lunch and a "girls gossip" kind of day. I don't, as a rule, do readings for friends. Mixing mediumship with friendship isn't a good idea in my experience. But, as with any good rule, there is always the exception and this was it. Dawn was really struggling with life so I offered to do her a mini reading using the Tarot cards (not my usual way of working). I clearly remember the feeling of one of the cards, it had a powerful vibration, I described to Dawn a gentleman now in the Spirit world being very close, around her. I described him as being a very significant guiding force in her life and a source of inspiration to her. I said he was a gentleman born under the sign of

Scorpio, all the time she was nodding but saying nothing. Then, there was a very distinctive smell and a taste developed in my mouth of petrol (at first I thought it was paraffin) however; it was the taste that was more prominent than the smell. I was able to describe the way the gentleman passed to Spirit, no pain, and no discomfort just a drifting into heavenly sleep.

I knew the man was a very close relative or friend of Dawn's, but I didn't know exactly who he was. She told me "that's my dad", she was very subdued and received the information very calmly, and I guess she was shocked at what I had felt from the cards. After all, she had expected to get her life sorted out, but instead we had made spiritual contact with her father. She had no hesitation in telling me how he had taken his life; he had started up a lawn mower engine in the bedroom. He had simply lain down and gone to sleep. I was able to tell Dawn that Adrian - her father had experienced a pleasant and as peaceful a passing as a person could wish for.

Before I tell you more I just want to reassure you that from my experience of working with Spirits, the moment of physical death is nothing to fear, neither do we "die" alone. Even if we are physically alone, spiritually we are not.

My own mum died in April 1986 after a 19-year battle with cancer. One thing that helped me deal with her passing to Spirit was that I knew she did not fear death. From being a teenager we spoke about it often, she was the one that used to say, "no one ever comes back and tells us what it's like". I never understood her saying that because, as a young woman, before she married my dad, she used to attend séances and "table rapping" sessions at a farmhouse in Astley, near Manchester, with a group of friends. I knew these were successful, so I did wonder why the denial?

As she got older she experienced many occurrences of a spiritual and psychic nature, she just stopped saying it, she found she couldn't after her experiences. The main event that made her "change her tune" was the period of Poltergeist activity that we lived through as a family. To my knowledge, everyone was affected except my dad. The activity happened when my younger sister was 13 and it really was horrendous. It made my mum think twice about chanting such a statement, but believe me; it would have made anyone push any doubts they had about the paranormal, out of the window. (I will come back to this in a separate chapter later on in the book).

In November 1985 mum told me that she had been disturbed in the night. She woke up with a strong feeling of a presence in the room, she opened her eyes and very clearly saw the head and torso of a man, as he appeared at the foot of her bed. She recognised him immediately as her father, she told me they looked at each other for a while, then he said, "I'm coming for you Annie" after which he just disappeared.

Next day she told me what she had seen and heard. She was clearly disturbed by the incident, I did my best to reassure her, but I fear it fell on stony ground. Even though mum had not been well for some months, I would not have thought she was getting ready to die, how wrong I was, the following April she passed to Spirit.

The cancer that had been controlled for all those years had spread throughout her body. She had a tremendously difficult last few days, thankfully she spent the last couple of hours sleeping, and she looked extremely fragile but more comfortable than she had for days. Suddenly she opened her eyes, very slowly turned her head and cast her eyes over everyone at the bedside, but was she really looking at us? Then she closed them again and slipped away.

The afternoon before she died, a good friend and colleague whom you have met earlier in this book, Jim Walker, came to the hospital to talk and spend some time with me. He told me the end would be soon, "around her bed will be three James's, they are coming for her". By ten past six that afternoon she was gone. When she had looked around, had she seen the family or had she seen James her father, James her father-in-law and James her brother-in-law who had been her first love? I felt happier to believe that at that moment, it was the latter three she saw. I hated the thought of her having to make that "journey" to the Spirit world alone, I know this sounds silly, but I thought, "she's not a well travelled lady, she could get lost".

A few days later Jim came to see me at home, he wanted to chat to offer me some assurance. He had some spiritual messages for me, he told me that the three James's had escorted her and she had arrived safely in the Spirit world. She was so tired of this life and more than ready to pass over, that it was only a short time before she "woke up" in the Spirit world. When she did, she asked for a cup of tea. At first she didn't realise she was in the Spirit world, the first realisation was when she noticed she was pain-free. These messages, plus a lot more, gave me such comfort. In my work I have comforted a lot of people, by passing on messages, now it was my turn to be comforted. Probably for the first time in my life, I needed, rather than wanted, a message from Spirit, after all it isn't every day that you lose a parent.

It is my opinion, that death is worse for the people left behind, than for the person who passes over. We are the ones left picking up the pieces, whether they are physical, mental or emotional. It would seem that the new Spirit, has everything to gain but I do believe a period of adjustment and acceptance is needed for the Spirit as well as the bereaved.

Chapter Fourteen

Just Passing Through

I have never ceased to be amazed and excited by the accounts of spiritual and psychic experiences that have been shared with me by clients, friends and family. I want to share with you now a group of experiences that happened within a few minutes or hours of a physical death.

It is a wonderfully reassuring thought that as many of our Spirit friends tell us, "We go to sleep then wake-up in the Spirit world". Well, I'm convinced that is how it is for many. I gathered together these accounts demonstrating how some Spirits do make a detour on their journey to the Spirit world, it is as though they have to visit someone or a special place, maybe for the last time, before they make a full transition into the Spirit world.

Squires Lane in Tyldesley, near Manchester, was a lovely place to grow up in. A quiet lane which reached out into fields and farmland, accessed by a road beneath a railway bridge, it was a little world of its own. There it was safe and comfortable, but people were very "small minded" as I was to discover as I got older. On the opposite side of the road lived a young man, Robert. As with most people in any small community we were aware of each other but not friends. 1973 was to change all that, Robert and his friends started to associate with my brother and sister and me, but only in a "friendly from a distance" sort of way. I think it must have been the magic age of 16 and of mopeds and 50 cc: motorcycles that brought everyone together.

As the months went by something very special emerged from this group friendship. A boyfriend/girlfriend relationship developed between Robert and my younger sister. He was 16 she was 15. Yes, they were young, but both of them extremely mature for their years, they fell in love. My younger sister once said to me, "Because we were young, people (parents mainly) didn't take us seriously".

The earthly love affair was extremely short-lived. In December of 1973, Robert discovered a lump on his left shoulder. An immediate appointment at the doctors was made for him and he was referred for an x-ray the very next day. At teatime his mum received a call from the hospital; the x-ray showed an abnormality and investigations were necessary. Investigations revealed bone cancer that was at a very advanced stage, the amputation of his arm and shoulder blade was advised by the consultant. This was done and I will never forget how brave Robert was. I feel he suffered dreadfully, both with pain and emotionally, but to his friends he never showed it. Robert thought the operation would make him better, but his mum knew from the start that he would die. The surgery was to make Robert more comfortable; it was only a matter of time before the cancer broke through the bone again.

He made a wonderful recovery from the operation; he was home a couple of weeks later. This was the period of time that drew Robert and my sister together. When he wasn't feeling well, she would "bunk off" school to be with him. It must have been done instinctively, knowing that he wouldn't be around for very long. She knew it was wrong to skip school, but did so anyway, doing what she thought was right at the time. Unknown to her, time was very short. One dreadful day in February Robert discovered another lump, as soon as he showed his mum she knew that this was it, the moment that she had been warned about, and had dreaded, had arrived.

It wasn't long before his friends guessed that Robert was going to die. He wasn't told, but I feel it wasn't long before he knew, deep inside. Looking back to that time, we all knew but no one wanted to acknowledge the fact that this was happening. All the hiding of emotions and pretending that nothing was wrong made it a much more difficult time than if we had been able to be more open with our thoughts and feelings. I've learned, over the years, that people do what they think is right at the time. I hope that when my time to pass-on comes, I'll be able to talk about it and prepare, to me this is a valuable part of the process.

On the 18th of April 1974 at 11.20 a.m. Robert passed away very peacefully. He was so brave, hiding all the pain and anguish to save the feelings of others. When Robert passed away, my sister was at home; she had slept in late that morning, after a very restless night. She went into the bathroom to wash. As she leaned over the basin, she was aware of a strong tug on the bottom of her nightdress; this stopped her in her tracks. She finished her toiletries and then went downstairs to find mum. Very calmly she said "Robert has died, I just know" then she told Mum what had happened. She made a note of the time which was 11.25 a.m. It wasn't very long before Robert's mum came to the house with the sad news. When she asked, "What time had Robert died?" "11.20" was the reply. This was one young man who didn't take the straight road to the Spirit world, he had to call off and say goodbye to someone he loved very much.

When my mum passed to the Spirit world on April 15th 1986 at ten past six in the evening. The family members who were at her bedside all had some tea made by the nursing staff. Then we returned to the accommodation provided for us by the hospital - a large Portacabin. This had been a home-from-home in the waiting time leading to her passing, but now it was time to gather up all our belongings and go home.

We were all very quiet as we went about our business. There had been a lot of tears shed during those last few days, the predominant feeling amongst us then was relief; the suffering was over. Suddenly the silence was broken by the radio switching itself on. At first there

106

were looks of shock and disbelief among us, then we smiled, one of us said, "It's her!" This was typical of mum, she was a joker in life and this was just the sort of thing she would do. Probably, in her way she was trying to cheer us up, or break the tension and ease the stress we were feeling. It suited us, at that moment, to believe it was she. Mum, has let us know through a medium that she went to sleep then woke up in the Spirit world asking for a cup of tea. If this was not actually her switching the radio on, it was someone. Could it have been one of the three James's who had passed through on her behalf to let us know that she was on her way and was safe?

The week before mum went into hospital for the last time, she had spent at my home. She was very weak and needed constant care. My father wasn't a well man, so the family agreed this was the best action to take. I tried to whet her appetite with tasty food, in order to build her strength. It was quite difficult, as nothing seemed to appeal. She had always been a lover of tinned salmon, so I bought some especially for her, however, before she could eat this, she was taken back into hospital, having taken a turn for the worse.

On returning home after mum's passing, I went upstairs and into my back bedroom, the room was filled with the smell of tinned salmon, I feel it had been intensified so that I could not misinterpret or dismiss the smell. "Come up here", I shouted downstairs to my sister. When she did I asked her "What can you smell?" To which she replied, "tinned salmon". I interpreted this as mum having called in to remind me that she never had her salmon sandwiches!

Sometimes the "just passing through" occurrences aren't as pleasing or as friendly as the ones I have just told you about. One of my clients, told me about the day his grandmother passed to Spirit. They had not been particularly close, but he had always respected her and helped her when he could. The last few weeks of her life had been spent in hospital and he had made a number of visits to see her; this had pleased her very much, she had told him so. This is his account of the events that took place.

"It was a normal Sunday evening, we had eaten tea and washed up. Suddenly the cat leaped into the air, she was normally a very placid cat, but this day she was hissing and whining. She ran at full speed across the room and crawled underneath the dresser. I attempted to entice her from underneath but she just screamed at me. She was extremely distressed; her legs were stretched out rigidly with her claws protruding. She was ready to rip the hand off anyone who attempted to get too near her".

My client told me "We didn't have a clue what was happening, all we knew was that something had *spooked her* and only she knew what that was. There was a noticeable change in the atmosphere, the lounge had grown chilly and there was a sensation of *time standing still*. After a few minutes, the room became calm again, the temperature rose, but the cat stayed in hiding for a couple of hours".

Later in the evening my client's dad came to tell them that Grandma had died. My client told me the he and his wife looked at each other, but said nothing. He asked at what time the lady died, the time given by his dad was a few minutes earlier than the event that had taken place in the lounge. Suddenly it all made sense; they always said that they had a psychic cat, but on this occasion she had excelled. They were convinced that the two events were related. "Grandma was just passing through to say goodbye to a special relative, the cat obviously didn't approve!"

This event does sound very spooky, I'm very sure the Spirits don't ever want to scare us. They do what they have to do in order to be recognised. On this occasion, if the cat had not been in the house, I think it is highly likely that she would have passed through without anyone being aware of her. My client himself is extremely sensitive to spiritual presence, so he may have got a tingle or that shiver which is often referred to as "someone walking over one's grave", I wonder if he would have realised how significant that feeling was? Cats and dogs are extremely sensitive to spiritual presence and they react in different ways, sometimes calmly, sometimes not!

Many people have had, and will continue to experience spiritual presence when someone has just passed over. These experiences create in us feelings ranging from those of joy and comfort, right across the spectrum to those of fear and distress. People often ask me "what does it mean when .... happens?" I rarely have an answer; experiences are as unique as the people themselves. There aren't any hard and fast rules. As "earthlings" we each perceive and interpret messages differently from the next person. I believe that the messages and experiences are given in the same manner. So, if one person sees a blue light flashing on a wall in their home, then their next-door neighbour sees the same thing. The reasons for it are, more likely than not, very different. Maybe, by now, you can appreciate what a difficult job being a working medium is. People think we have all the answers, but we haven't, every day is a new and learning experience.

Chapter Fifteen

Preparing to pass over

I think the most popular request from clients is "don't tell me anything bad". What they usually mean is "don't tell me if I'm going to die or if anyone around me is. What people don't realise is that my information has been "censored at source". All information must be passed on; it isn't for me to keep for myself. Spirits know what the individual can take; they also know what they need to know. That is why, so often, sad news is disguised on the day of the sitting. By the time the person would benefit from knowing the bad news, the meaning of the information given at the sitting would have unfolded. It can be likened to a cryptic clue.

Death is a big part of life and I feel there are many situations where it is advantageous to know what lies ahead, if we're going to experience a personal loss. It gives time for physical and mental preparations, the tying up of loose ends and much more.

In an earlier chapter I told you about the visit my grandfather made to my mum, telling her that he was coming to take her to Spirit. I took that forewarning and used it to its fullest extent. I hope I was discrete about it. I made sure that I did things that I wouldn't have done, had I not had the warming. I spent more time with her. We talked much more, opening up conversations into areas I wouldn't normally have done; intimate subjects, delving into the past in more depth and detail than I ever did in the past. I felt I needed to know about my ancestors, things that only she would know. I was genuinely interested and I knew within a short time, my chance would be gone, so it was now or never! The thing that annoyed me about all this was that I had been thinking of asking these questions for years, and like many other people, I had put it off and off. Then to realise that time was running out. I had no time to waste, act or remain in the dark forever.

This was a great treat for mum; she loved to talk about the past and the family, but was rarely given the chance apart from making comments in passing. The "floodgates" opened and I loved it. I secretly recorded names and details; I gained knowledge from her. I always felt it was a therapy; not just for her, but for me.

I can remember being a little girl of 8 and clearly recall having thoughts and dreads about the day when my mum would die and leave me. As I write this, it seems a morbid thought for a child to have, but I can't make any excuses for having it. Just that maybe I started my mental preparation all that time ago. I have never been a stranger to death, as I grew up there always seemed to be someone dying. Some of those people were parents of people I knew. This reinforced my thoughts, that one day it would be my turn. I make a point of this because I have met so many people who never allow that thought in their minds. Their parents would "live forever". Then the terrible reality of finding out that it's not true has proved too much for them to handle, way beyond grief.

When the day finally arrived and my mum passed to Spirit. Yes, I was sad and upset but I was prepared too. I feel both the long-term and the short-term preparations played a huge part in this. From the age of eight years old I knew she would die one day. In November of 1985, I knew it would be soon. None of this made the pain any less but it did speed my passage through the grief process. I just want to compare this with the loss of my dad. I was devastated when he died, as I wasn't as prepared. It sounds very naive, but I chose to believe that he would live forever, regardless of the fact that all the signs were there.

Many clients are like me; they prefer to know if there is to be a death in the reasonably near future. Those who say it and mean it will usually get to know. Feedback tells me that "knowing" was a great asset to them.

It isn't always the case that a client is told the name of the person, who will pass to Spirit, only that it will happen. Two main reasons for this come to mind. Firstly, the client needs in general to assess their own lives and review their relationships. It could be that they have become too isolated or selfish. Maybe they should look at their lives and ask themselves the question "would I have any regrets about the quality of my relationship with...?", presuming those people who come to mind were to die tomorrow. Then when that question has been truthfully answered, are there any bridges that need building? Not knowing exactly who will be physically leaving their life, can work as a great healer in general.

The second answer is much simpler; the client just couldn't handle knowing exactly who. One such example is a lady called Enid, a client of mine for many years. After many regular sittings a good relationship formed and it felt as though we had been through "thick and thin" together. I want to talk about one sitting that I did for her. It was clouded with sadness. I gave her information, but at the time she didn't understand. In the reading was the name of Terry on the earth, which didn't have any significance either on the day.

Enid came to see me a few months later dreadfully upset. She told me that her stepdaughter's baby, who was only a few weeks old, had died. It had been a cot death. She continued to tell me that her stepdaughter had been a little undecided about the baby's name. After a long period of indecision, she finally chose a name, which everyone thought she was happy with. Unknown to Enid, just before the baby passed away, his name was changed to Terry. Enid only discovered this when she received a phone call with news of the baby's death.

Enid told me that the detail in the reading, about the name, had shaken her rigid. Being told that there was to be sadness had alerted

Enid to prepare for a sad event. Even though she was devastated by the little boy's death, she gained consolation and comfort from the sitting. She knew that the Spirits had been making preparations to receive the baby back into their world.

I have no doubts, as I have explained earlier in the book, that knowing both my mum and then my dad would soon be physically leaving me, helped me to prepare for these events. Heather, yet another long-standing client of mine had a very close relationship with her father. They were very like-minded, which made for a close relationship as well as an interesting one.

Two years before her father passed to Spirit, I told Heather what was going to happen. I was very gentle in my delivery and she accepted the message very well. After the spiritual work was done, we talked. I told her what she could expect in the way of changed behaviour, things he would say and do. I advised her that they were all part of the "gearing down process", which can lead us all to a "good death" and a peaceful passing into the Spirit world.

Not everyone gets a chance to go through this process, for example, sudden deaths; although I do feel there's a preparation, but at a subconscious and unconscious level and very different from the "gearing down process" best described as "having one foot on the earth and one foot in the Spirit world". At this stage there seems to be a lot of spiritual free floating; trips to the Spirit world and back of course, visits to the past and also receiving Spirit visitors which is very common.

Heather came back for a sitting a few months after her father passed over; she thanked me for helping her. She said that knowing what to expect from her father and the advice on how to deal with everything, had helped her to understand him, she was therefore able to make the best of the time available.

Losing someone as special as a parent, no matter how young or how old you are, is usually a dreadful experience. Having faith and knowledge that life doesn't stop with the physical death is a tremendous asset; it helps first with the dealing, then the healing.

Have you ever spent time with a person who is dying? It is, no doubt, a very difficult thing to do, but it can be one of the most amazing and rewarding experiences to have. From an early age I have had people relate to me many stories of dying relatives and friends who had been in conversation with an "invisible person" just days or hours before they have passed over. I have had a lots of nurse clients during my career. They are a wealth of information in this department, having seen this take place on numerous occasions. Some of their accounts have been extremely emotional and reassuring. Before I fully understood about the after-life, my friend's mother told me of such an experience, I was about 13 at the time. I thought it made so much sense, it just felt natural, there didn't seem to be anything "iffy" or "far fetched" about it.

I believe from what I have witnessed and from listening to the accounts of very rational human beings, that part of the preparation process includes the dying person experiencing spiritual encounters. Some of these encounters, I have learned, take place in their sleep state. These "meetings" can't just be passed off as dreams. For some there is a one-off experience, for others, like my dad who had regular morning visits, it is ongoing until they pass over. I would like to say that for most people it's a "death-bed" experience and a privilege to witness for those lucky enough to be present.

Visits from Spirits, to people who are going to pass to Spirit, are not always warm and cosy as my mum to my dad. This is a prime example, for many years I used to work in Leigh in Lancashire. I became very familiar with many faces in the town, even though I didn't know them personally or even get to know their names. There were two young men who worked on a local market; they had been there so long they were almost part of the fixtures and fittings.

Very sadly one of them, John, was killed in a car accident. The whole market community was devastated by the tragedy. One of my clients who became a friend and who I only met some years after the tragedy told me that in the months that followed the accident, a few of the market traders sensed the presence of the man who had been killed.

Sometime after the accident, a good friend of John's called Andrew went to make some tea in the communal kitchen in the market hall. He came out of the kitchen quicker than he had gone in; he looked very pale. My friend said to him "what on earth is the matter? You look as though you have seen a ghost". Andrew told her that he had seen John. Now anyone who encountered Andrew would have known him as a kind of laid back and fun loving sort of guy. Ghosts and spiritual matters would have been ridiculed or dismissed by him, however all that changed in an instant once he had seen John. (This is usually the case, once the person has "seen", there's no going back to old beliefs).

I can't recall the exact period of time, although I feel it was around 12 months after Andrew had seen John's Spirit, that he was also killed in a car accident. I feel this was a classic case of two mates on the earth, one moved on, then he came to lead the way for the other to follow. It sounds simple, maybe this is my fantasy, but I don't feel it's too far from the truth.

I must say to everyone, please don't panic if you see a Spirit it is not necessarily a sign of your own death. I feel that there are visions and visions. One thing is for sure, Spirits appear for something, some are joyous experiences and bring comfort and reassurance, and others are more intense or serious. They are to warn us of an event, or difficult situation.

The time I spent with my father during his last two days and nights was, from a spiritual point of view, "a magical time". On Saturday afternoon, the 16th of April 1988, dad's health took a tremendous turn for the worse. He hadn't been well for a few weeks and from the things he had been talking about and his actions, I knew, from a professional point of view that he was "gearing down". However, when he took his "nose dive", I was very upset. There was a moment when, no matter how professional and knowledgeable I was concerning this area, all reason went out of the window, I was only human and I feared what was about to happen.

He hated doctors, during the past two years since my mum had passed to Spirit, he had made my sisters and me promise faithfully that we would never let them take him away to hospital. He told us, "when I die I want to be in my own bed with my Long Johns on!" We did promise and when the time came, we were able to keep that promise. Regardless of the pressures we were under from the stream of medical visitors he had over his last couple of days, he was not sent to hospital.

His last weekend felt like the longest two days and nights of my life. The days just seemed to go on forever, he slept most of the time. Then the night time came and things were very different; I was dozing in the chair and dad started to talk. I couldn't make out what he was saying, so I said "what do you want dad?" "I'm not talking to you," he said. I was a little taken aback, because he spoke so sharply, then I asked him who he was talking to, he told me it was his dad, and he asked me to keep quiet.

The conversation went on for a few minutes then he lay down to rest. What I thought was so amazing was, this man was so full of pain in and around his stomach, that he could hardly move. When the Spirit of my grandfather entered the room, he raised himself up onto the pillow and greeted him with a smile.

Granddad was the first of a series of visitors, some he greeted with a smile others he reached out his hand to greet. This procession of spiritual visitors lasted throughout the Saturday night; some of the names were familiar to my sister and me, we either knew of them from the past or they had still been around in our childhood. One of dad's old friends who had been in Spirit for at least 20 years came to talk over old times. They had both worked as butchers since they were boys. One very emotional moment was when my dad's first wife Jane came to visit. At that time my brother Danny was sitting on the side of the bed, after a short conversation he reached out to Danny, cupped his face in his hands and kissed him on the mouth. I felt Jane was sitting in front of Danny, but not as a solid mass, when dad reached out for her he took hold of Danny instead. Whatever happened, it was all so emotional.

Many people had told me about this sort of "happening", but I could never have imagined the beautiful feelings and emotions surrounding it. So much happened that night, it is difficult to pinpoint highlights, but I can tell you of a very funny part of the experience. Dad was resting after receiving a bunch of "visitors". This was about four in the morning, Marion (my older sister) was sitting on his bed, all was very quiet and calm, then dad raised his head and he said, "there's someone knocking on the door". We did nothing apart from look at each other, as we could hear nothing. Then dad got a little annoyed and repeated himself, he leaned forward and tapped Marion on the arm saying, "Go and open the door". After looking at me for some kind of reassurance, she did. Dad's face lit up, "it's Jimmy Bleakley" he said; this was a dear old friend from the past. With him came two other men, I recognised one from the gist of the conversation as being a man who had died in a motor cycle accident, when both he and dad were in their '20s.

The whole thing was marvellous, what a privilege to see such a spectacle, I remember feeling like an intruder, this was a very private time for dad, I did leave the room on a few occasions partly to give him privacy, partly because I was in tears with emotion.

The Sunday night was much quieter from a spiritual point of view, only a couple of spiritual visitors. At 3.45 a.m. dad suffered a massive heart attack, the emergency doctor came, gave him a pain killing injection and he fell into a coma. I could feel the Spirits gathering close around him, I knew he was in their care from that moment on. This gave me some time to concentrate on my own feelings, and I realised I wasn't handling this very well from an emotional point of view. At 3.40 p.m. on the 18th of April dad passed to Spirit. I never knew which of those Spirits were gathered around at the final stage, although I guess that Mum did come to him at the end. I just want to comment that this is the second time that the 18th of April has appeared in this book. The first time was the day my sister's boyfriend Robert passed. We found it unbelievable that two men, whom she had loved so much, had left the earth on the same day.

1991 brought yet another tragedy to our family. In September of that year, my sister in law, Irene lost her long battle with cancer. I spent as much time as I could with her in the last few weeks of her life. We talked at length and in great depth about the Spirit world and life after death. She told me, in an almost apologetic voice, that up to a couple of years earlier she did not believe in the Spirit world. Death meant the end of everything. It was an experience that she had a couple of years previously that changed her mind. She and my brother had owned a number of Siamese cats, greatly loved by them.

116

One day she saw the Spirit of one of her late cats running upstairs at home. This started to be a regular occurrence and not just for her, my brother Louis also saw him. That was also his belief system in tatters!

Shortly before Irene became ill, she had been shopping in the local supermarket. As she stepped outside, she looked across the road, to her great surprise she saw her father-in-law, my dad, just standing looking at her. She told me he was very smart and looking in good health. They had a few moments of eye contact and then he disappeared. This was the first of a series of sightings, as she told me about it, she was clearly thrilled. The impression she gave me was of a "child at Christmas" a mixture of magic mixed with reality. It made me smile a little because she knew what my job had been for a number of years, yet here she was trying to convince me that there was an afterlife! It's a very common reaction from a "new convert".

She had seen Dad a number of times, but the visits stopped as she became more ill, however the cats seemed to appear daily. She went into a Manchester hospital to have some laser treatment on her hip. She wasn't very hungry so the sandwiches that had been given to her for tea were placed on the windowsill behind her. She told me she felt a presence, when she looked around, she saw two of her beloved spiritual cats sitting staring at them, this prompted her to eat the sandwiches. She knew they were Spirit cats yet, as she emphasised "they were so real, so *there*" I think that final statement says it all!

2003 brought about yet another huge blow to my system, the "death" of Irene's husband, my brother Lou. He was diagnosed in the March with secondary bone cancer with unknown primary. He asked Martin and me to move in with him for the time he had left, he never really accepted the doctors' diagnosis; insisting that they had made a mistake, yet deep down he did know that his life was on a timer, he did speak to me about it, however this didn't stop him thinking long-term and even making plans for the future.

His condition deteriorated rapidly, what lay ahead in the time until he passed to Spirit, both for him and for us, is really too distressing to talk about and I really feel he would rather I didn't. He would say, "It's history".

I feel that he asked me to be with him to help him prepare for his passing to Spirit. He knew in his heart he was not ready to go, in fact he was terrified of going, he hung on to life for longer than anyone of the experts thought he would, or indeed could. They were absolutely amazed at how long he "survived". There were a couple of incidents I want to tell you about, which occurred during the last couple of weeks of his life. In Lou's bedroom was an armchair on which we placed a spare duvet. He said to Martin, "move that bloody duvet off that chair, I keep thinking there is someone sitting there!" Martin moved it immediately; I said to him privately, "That's because there bloody is someone there!" I am sure this was Irene, just waiting for him; but he wasn't having any of that stuff.

Another day, Martin was helping him from the bathroom to his bedroom; the door to the second bedroom was open, he looked in, and then said to Martin, "Is there an Indian lady in there?" He clearly saw someone sitting on the bed.

The house was heavy with spiritual visitors during those weeks. This became more intense the nearer we got to his passing. A few days before, I was preparing food in the kitchen; suddenly there was a continual "tap-tap-tap" on the door, which was mainly glass. I sensed it was Irene, it sounded as if she was tapping on the glass with her heavy ring-clad finger. Another day there was a heavy rapping on the front door, at the time I was standing in the hall. Startled by the noise, I went straight to the door and opened it, and found nobody! I have heard of this happening to other people when a death was imminent in a household. Some call it "The knock of death". I just took it as a forewarning and to prepare myself.

Lou passed to Spirit at 9.30 a.m. on Saturday 13th July. He suffered some sort of trauma, a stroke or haemorrhage at about 5.15 a.m. The nurses came and made him comfortable and he never moved after

that, he was in a coma. Just before 9.30 Martin was seated by the bed holding Lou's hand, I stood behind him with my hands on his shoulders, behind me was someone from the Spirit world holding my shoulders; we were in a chain. I said to Martin, "This is strange, you are holding Lou, I'm holding you and someone is holding me!" Lou gasped his final breath at that moment, he was finally free of the pain and the loneliness he had endured since Irene passed over, he was finally free.

Louis and Irene as I like to imagine them, happy together in the Spirit world; as they were in the late 1950s, soon after they met.

I have had a number of readings since this happened, from my trusty medium Joseph. I have all the evidence I need that Lou is with

Irene, he's happy; he confirmed that I helped him prepare to pass over. I was told that he had stayed with us for a few hours after his physical death because he didn't want to leave us, also that it was our dad who actually came for him that beautiful sunny morning, naturally, he was his child, his eldest son. For weeks beforehand he kept telling me that he would be OK when the sunny weather came. I believe that he was, a self-fulfilling prophecy!

Louis the master butcher with his wife Irene (the butcher's assistant!) shortly before he retired.

Chapter Sixteen

Disaster

Many people have premonitions of forthcoming events, especially tragedy and disaster. Some see this in their dreams, some people get "clairvoyant flashes" whilst others simply "feel it in their water", as one person described it to me. I have only ever experienced one premonition of a disaster (apart from seeing them in readings for other people). I awoke one morning; I was alone in bed. My husband was downstairs watching TV. When he came back upstairs I asked him how many people had been killed in the jumbo jet aircraft. "What crash" he asked. "The one I have just heard on the news as I awoke" I replied. There hadn't been a crash that morning, however, the following morning, he woke me up to tell me "now there's been a crash". It was somewhere in Asia; I apologise for the lack of factual detail; as for some reason it hasn't stayed with me. The point I am really trying to make is, how vivid the premonition was, I was obviously still asleep when I thought I could hear the report on the TV. What this did for me was to give me some insight into how it feels for other people when they experience disaster premonitions. I find it acceptable as part-and-parcel of my job; outside that boundary, I must say I didn't really care for it at all!

For some of the people I have met, premonitions of this kind are a way of life. This includes friends as well as clients. Before I continue to share with you a selection of these amazing experiences, I would like to say that I don't understand why certain people get to know about these events beforehand, I know even less what they are meant to do with the information when they get it. But people do know about forthcoming events. For thousands of years, people have been seeing the future. By now I would've thought the world would be open-minded - maybe it's happening - but I feel there is a long way to go.

It is quite common for people to "see" or "know" things, but not realise at the time, that it is a premonition. It registers, and then it is forgotten almost instantly or at least from the conscious mind. When the event occurs, there is instant recall, and the person may say something like "I knew that would happen!" Quite often nobody believes them.

My friend Jenny, whom you met earlier in the book, was one such person who "suffered" these disaster premonitions. For Jenny they were not a "flash in the pan" and then forgotten. They were taken very much on-board and, more often than not, they were discussed with her husband Barry. Together they would wait for the event to take place, after that there was often a sense of relief. At least the waiting was over, but that was mixed with feelings of sadness at the loss of life in these accidents or disasters. Later in the chapter, I want to share with you some of the intense premonitions that Jenny experienced. I feel that the timing of my writing this chapter is very relevant, in a few days it will be the second anniversary of her passing to Spirit (30.8.97). I feel she's close by and is helping me write this book. She would want to help other people, who feel inflicted as she did, with this "gift".

A person with whom I was discussing the subject once asked me "does this only happen to a certain type of person, such as a pessimistically natured or depressed person, or someone with mental problems?" My answer had to be "no". Most people I have met, including myself, are very positive natured, with an optimistic outlook to life in general. Maybe the common denominator is that each of them is highly intuitive and spiritually open-minded.

Tony and Susan are two business people who have been clients of mine for many years. On one of his visits, Tony told me about one of his wife Susan's premonitions. At the time she experienced it, neither of them understood, they didn't realise they were being given a warning of a terrible disaster that was to happen shortly. The year was 1984. Susan and Tony went to bed as normal, in the middle of the night, Susan awoke, and she could smell burning, very strongly. After a while, she woke Tony and asked him if he could smell the "burning", he couldn't. Then it became very distinctive, like burning rubber or a chemical smell.

Susan couldn't rest, she asked Tony to go downstairs to check the new microwave that they had bought only a few days earlier. He did this and then reported back to her that all was well. But all wasn't well with Susan, she sent him back downstairs to check all the plugs and sockets in the house, he couldn't find a problem anywhere. Eventually they were able to get back to sleep. The next day the news hit the headlines; there had been a dreadful disaster in Bhopal, India. There had been an accident at a chemical factory, a gas explosion; thousands of people were injured in the surrounding area, blinded by the fumes from the factory. The smell from the explosion was similar to the smell of burning rubber - the smell that Susan had experienced. This is a classic example of a disaster premonition.

The next example is one I'm sure everyone will remember, as it is closer to home. On the 15th April 1989 there was a terrible disaster at the Hillsborough Stadium in Yorkshire in which 95 people were killed and 120 people were injured. A couple of weeks before this event I did a sitting for a lady. In the sitting I saw an image of thousands of bunches of flowers, it looked like a sea of colour. I wasn't sure what it meant; I thought it was probably a festival or horticultural show. How wrong can one be! How wrong it is for mediums to try and interpret spiritual messages. I did tell my client that this scene would be very relevant in the near future and that the message that came with it was "not to worry."

A couple of weeks later, Saturday 15th April, my client heard the news of the terrible tragedy at the Hillsborough Stadium. It was particularly relevant too, as both her husband and son had gone there that day. For hours she was frantic with worry, she didn't know if the men were alive or dead. At first she was too upset to think straight, then the words from the reading came into her mind, "don't worry". Later in the afternoon she received a call from her husband to say they were OK. Over the next few days, thousands of floral tributes flooded into the Stadium forming this "sea of colour" that I had seen in the sitting.

When I did the sitting, I didn't have any idea what I was talking about. If I had, would anyone have listened to me?

Through doing my spiritual work for many years, I have formed a number of personal philosophies and theories although I must say that I still don't have the "secret of life!" One of my theories is that there's almost always a warning (a physical sign), in some shape or form, before a tragedy or disaster. More often than not, we don't see, or we choose not to see, them. I'm a great believer and promoter of personal and worldwide awareness. I'm tempted to shoot off at a tangent here but I won't, I'll leave that for you to do. Predictions are usually "The last straw", as if the Spirits are stepping in to shake us into seeing what lies ahead.

In recent years there have been a number of air crashes, but the two that I want to talk about happened in our country. The first one is Lockerbie on the 22nd December 1988. The second was Kegworth, Leicestershire on the 9th of January 1989, the plane, a British Midland, crashed beside the M1 motorway. We come back to my good friend Jenny Jones. In the later years of her life, she experienced some extraordinary predictions; both of these accidents were among them.

Jenny lived on the Staffordshire/Cheshire border on a smallholding on the top of a hill. This gave beautiful views of the surrounding countryside. She was very much an outdoor person and that is where she spent most of her time when she wasn't writing. One very cold, yet clear, day just a week or so before Christmas, Jenny was standing in her beloved donkey field. Everything was calm and clear, she told me her eyes were drawn towards the sky where she saw a blinding flash of light, just like an explosion, yet there was no noise. It was very hard to carry on looking, as the light was so bright it hurt her eyes. After a few seconds she was compelled to look up again, she said, "I know it sounds silly but my first thoughts were, that the sun had exploded".

After a few moments she gathered her senses and looked for the sun. It was still there, but in a completely different location, then she looked back at the blinding light, which just disappeared in an instant before her eyes.

Jenny had a very logical brain even though she was a great believer in spiritual and psychic matters. She did like to think about these matters for a while before she said anything to anyone. However, once processed she came to the conclusion that this was a "big thing" that was to come, even though she didn't understand what. More often than not, she would tell me once the prediction had occurred. But for some reason she told me about this one beforehand. The detail that she was very sure about, was that many people would be affected, their lives shattered by the event. There were only days to wait for the event to take place, a 747 jumbo jet exploded over Lockerbie in Scotland.

The British Midland crash at the side of the M1 in 1989 was "given" to her differently. The only person who knew about this beforehand was Barry, her husband. Jenny told me that this one came to her in snatches over a period of time. The clairvoyant pictures were extremely vivid. She knew the plane had "British" in the name of the company, a road would be involved and roughly 50 people would die.

Expectation of the event hung over her for week after week, she felt in the constant state of waiting for something to happen, all the time the feelings got stronger as the time of the disaster approached.

The day it happened, she was sitting with Barry, watching the news. When the pictures flashed up on the screen, she just grabbed Barry's hand and wept, partly with relief that the waiting was over, and partly with sadness at such a tragic loss of life.

Barry once told me that she always seemed to know about one thing or another. Sadly the shock of Jenny's sudden departure to the Spirit world seems to have blotted a lot of these details from his mind, so I can only give you these examples, plus one more tragedy, which I know caused her tremendous stress. A large ship, which was sailing on the China Sea, caught fire and sank. There was a huge loss of life in this disaster. In the premonitions she could see the flames, and hear the screams of the people who were trapped inside the ship. After this event, she told me that she was sure that this accident could have been prevented. People had been negligent and careless.

Fires don't just happen, ferries like 'The Herald of Free Enterprise' involved in the Zebrugge disaster, don't just sink, neither do bombs just walk on-board planes. Human beings can be too careless or negligent. Premonitions, on the whole, are our spiritual friends pushing us to be more careful. Telling us we have overlooked something, or even that we are ignoring something that we shouldn't.

I just want to add a few thoughts that have sprung to mind today. The first skeleton draft of this book was written mainly in Sussex. Now I live in beautiful Shropshire in a historic market town called Much Wenlock, which proudly boasts a magnificent abbey ruin - Wenlock Priory. I was there last weekend, absorbing the atmosphere but also feeling sad for the abbey. What a series of disasters Henry VIII caused with the dissolution of the monasteries in the 16th century! I can't help wondering whether that disaster was foretold in any way or even recorded somewhere. I would imagine all the warning signs were there, but how could they have stopped it, or should I say stopped him? So much "food for thought" here, maybe we are coming to a time when those "in the know" must speak out. There will always be ridicule from the sceptics, but what the hell! If it saves just one life then it is worth speaking out. What is there to lose?

Chapter Seventeen

Amorous Spirits

There is one area of spiritual work that I have decided is definitely not my field. That is dealing with troubled or earthbound Spirits. I believe it is something that should be left to the experts, however, it has not stopped people contacting me for help with their problems or concerns connected with this area.

Even though I am a lot older and wiser than when I first started doing this work, I have to be honest and say, Poltergeist activity or Spirits that in general wish to cause disruption, do scare me. I may sound very sexist here, but I always felt that this was a man's job. Maybe that's because I consider myself weak and vulnerable at times, just right for the troubled soul to latch onto if I wasn't strong and hence cause myself more trouble than I could handle.

In the past it has been quite a regular occurrence to receive a phone-call from someone asking for my help. They usually had an exorcism in mind, or wanted me to investigate a house or building, which had paranormal activity on a day-to-day basis, which was affecting the quality of their daily life.

If I were asked for advice, then that's fine, I would refer them to an "Expert" such as my friend Jim Walker. Being a very strong character, this kind of work (ghost busting) suited him. People who knew me through my spiritual work often pushed me hard, but I always decline. I have a duty of care to myself first - ghost busting isn't on my agenda!

Not every spiritual experience is pleasant, as we have discussed already. Here are two accounts, relayed to me by clients of amorous spiritual visitors; the first account was from an Asian lady who came to see me some years ago. It was her first visit to me and we liked each other instantly, this helped, the reading set off to a good start. She was such an interesting and interested person; all aspects of the spiritual world caught her interest. She had been brought up as a Muslim, she had great respect for her faith but she told me she needed more. The Muslim religion teaches that life continues after death, we go to "Paradise" but that is it, no more contact, in other words that is the cut-off point. This lady believed strongly in the spiritual faith so she had readings to gain knowledge and help from the Spirits.

As I worked with her, regardless of the fact that she spoke openly with me, I sensed she was a very intense person; also that she was a person who had a secret. I tried to "know" her secret but I wasn't allowed to become privy to this. (The Spirits don't allow nosiness or gossip of any kind). So I moved on quickly and we covered a lot of areas. At the end of the reading, I asked her, as I always ask my clients, "are there any questions you would like to ask me?" unsurprisingly she said "yes". So, I sat back and listened to her intriguing story.

For a few months, Gemma had been having a Spirit visitor; he was a man and he always made his visit during the night. The first time he came, she felt a weight on the bed; this was someone lying beside her, with his arm across her stomach. She told me she could not see him, she just felt him. At first, that was all there was to it. She shared the bedroom with her sister; the visitor just came to lie with her.

Then, occasionally, her sister started to stay with a friend, and "this is where it all changed", she told me, "in what way?" I asked. She carried on to tell me that the Spirit had made love to her. I was the only person she had told because, apart from people thinking she was mentally unbalanced, if they had believed her, then they may have been shocked or disgusted. I reassured Gemma that this was not the first time I had been told of a situation like this. This reassured her and spurred her on to give me more details. The main problem was that she felt guilty. When I asked her why she felt guilt she told me, it was because she liked her Spirit lover so much, she never wanted him to stop visiting her. She described him is gentle and wonderful and when he left her, she felt amazing for days, so alive and happy.

I consulted my Spirit guides after our conversation. They told me that the Spirit was an earthbound soul (someone who had not made the transition to the Spirit world and remains on the earth but in Spirit form), a young man, who had been killed in a road accident with his fiancée. She had passed to the Spirit world but he had not, I didn't know why. He didn't realise his fiancée had made the transition, yet for some reason, unknown to us, he had attached himself to Gemma, she made him feel safe and loved.

My Spirits told me that now, he would make his way forward to the Spirit world, he would come to terms with the situation and he would be escorted over, to be with his old love.

All this conjured up an image in my mind of a team of "rescue workers". Similar to a mountain rescue team rushing out to bring someone safely home. Gemma was far from pleased, deeply saddened to be precise. It was not what she wanted to hear, but as I explained to her, that for her own long-term happiness, she had to "let him go".

The second amorous Spirit I want to tell you about is a "different kettle of fish" altogether. June, who had been a long-standing client of mine and for many years the best friend of Jean the "victim", brought this story to my door. As soon as these terrible occurrences began, June invited Jean to stay at her house until they could seek some professional help.

June approach me for help, but I knew I would have been out of my depth, so for her (or should I say Jean's) sake I recommended a medium in Manchester who was experienced in this sort of thing. I did however, want to know about the situation and she was more than willing to share the details.

Jean had lived alone for a number of years, she was very settled and extremely used to her own company in the house, so the moment the unwelcome "house guest" moved in, she noticed it. At first it was simply the feeling of not being alone, intrusive and slightly unnerving. The problems started when the Spirit kept touching her in intimate places. At first she felt afraid, then she convinced herself she was going mad. June told me, Jean was one of the sanest people she had ever met, if she said it was happening, then it was happening!

This stage lasted a couple of weeks, then came the dreadful night that forced Jean to move out of her home. She was woken abruptly from her sleep, pinned down on the bed by an invisible force, she could not move at all and she felt terrified. She could feel hands touching her body, she tried to scream but nothing came out. Suddenly she was flipped over onto her stomach; a terrible ordeal was taking place now. The Spirit forced himself into her and was having sex with her from the back. She said the ordeal seemed to go on forever, but in reality it was for only a few minutes. A few minutes that left her exhausted, distressed and terrified. She felt as though she had been raped, but the question was by whom? She couldn't tell anyone, there was no visible rapist or forensic evidence, who would believe such a story? Luckily for Jean, her friend believed her, and so did I. Help was sorted, and I heard later, that the "necessary" was done to free the earthbound Spirit and to make Jean's house feel like a home again.

I hope you'll read both of these accounts with interest, even for a firm believer in the Spiritual world; these are very hard to take in. They aren't common occurrences, especially not in this country (probably more common place in Africa) but they definitely do occur. I have used the most powerful examples that I've come across to demonstrate the physical presence and power that Spirits are capable of using. One was gentle and loving, yet very strong; the other was forceful and aggressive. For me, this goes to show that people don't really change. Just because they leave the earth brutal or violent, they won't become angels overnight. In both of these cases, the Spirit did not make a transition from this world to the next but remained trapped between two worlds - earthbound. I just want to say that, I feel sure it would take more than a successful passage into the Spirit world for this violent natured Spirit to become reformed and at peace with himself. What happens after passage is a mystery to me, apart from being told that we all have to face a review of our lives on earth – what a daunting thought!

Chapter Eighteen

Poltergeist Activity

I have to admit that while writing the last chapter, I felt quite affected by the experiences of the two ladies involved. As I have already admitted, I do get "spooked". Probably less easily than I used to, but enough to send a tingle up my spine when I hear something amazing or unusual.

I think I like being like this, it's a sure sign of having my feet on the ground and never getting blasé with all this "stuff".

Being mentally engrossed in the last chapter took me back in time to 1971 when I was 18. At that time I experienced strong feelings of fear; these related to a series of paranormal experiences. The time of year when all this began was November; I remember it as a particularly wet and dark month. The activities lasted for a period of two to three months, hard to be exact as it all fizzled away as quickly as it had started.

My brother, Danny, seemed to have the "Spirit seeing eyes" in our household during the time we were growing up. On a number of occasions he saw a Spirit lady walking across the landing. He would be terrified and would cry, or even scream out. My dad would take a dim view of this! He would reprimand Danny saying, "go to sleep" (easier said than done I remember).

In general we weren't strangers to things that "go bump in the night". But events of November 1971 were very different. When I say each member of the family, I don't include my dad, but the rest of us all witnessed or experienced a variety of different psychic occurrences. We kept most of it to ourselves when it first started, but that didn't last long. Life became unbearable in our house, so we had to talk to mum about it.

The worst experience for me was, sensing the presence of a Spirit, which I did not like. I had grown up with my dad's first wife Jane "in residence" from time to time. I didn't like it, but there wasn't a feeling of danger or threat with her; as there was with this presence. I would often attempt to go upstairs and after climbing 4 or 5 steps, do an about turn and usually "fly" down the stairs. You can imagine the noise, like "a herd of elephants" coming downstairs. Mum would shout, "what are you running for, you silly thing, you'll break your neck". At first I was too embarrassed to say why I had been running, I would make up stupid excuses like "I forgot something" or "I changed my mind" not that she believed me for one minute!

Up to now, my experiences don't sound like much, but they were scary enough for me. One that was also experienced by both my sister and my mum when sitting on the loo which was situated directly at the top of the stairs on the left; we each heard, on separate occasions, a very distinctive creak on the stairs. This came from the third step from the top, after the turn. This stair always made a noise when anyone stood on it, the occasions in question were when no one else was in the house or we were sure that no one else had come upstairs. It's human nature to call out "is that you mum?" Or whoever was expected. Of course there was no answer on these occasions!

At first I didn't just accept this, I searched the bedrooms, calling out for mum again, just in case she hadn't heard me. Then the fear of God came over me, commonly known as "the willies". I would then proceed to descend the stairs at the speed of light, risking life and limb. The final straw came when I was sitting on the loo and "someone" was trying to push the toilet door open. The second I realised it wasn't an "earthling" I jumped up and shot downstairs without finishing the business at hand. I had to give mum a full report; I couldn't put up with keeping it to myself anymore. She was wonderful, she understood, similar things had been happening to her too. The first thing she did was to escort me back to the loo. This was the first of many escorted visits to the toilet during the next couple of months, not just for me but for my younger sister and Danny too.

Mum told me she hadn't said anything because she hadn't wanted to scare us. It was the first time in my life that I understood the value of the saying "A problem shared is a problem halved"; at least it felt something like that to me. As you can appreciate, the situation was very difficult. Mum was very understanding, but dad would stand for none of this nonsense had he been told about it, but he wasn't, we kept it to ourselves and supported each other the best we could.

My younger sister, Danny and my mum had far more terrifying experiences than I did. One morning my younger sister woke up to find she was being pressed down into the bed, as she became more conscious she realised it wasn't a dream. She became more and more aware of an invisible hand on her hip holding her down; a second hand was on the side of her face. She could not move, she tried, with all her might to shout, "mum" for help; but nothing came out of her mouth. The longer it went on, the more distressed she became.

The traumatic experience lasted for a few minutes; eventually she managed to struggle and break herself free and then leaped up and made her way downstairs at the speed of wind. The experience reduced her to tears. What you must know is, that my younger sister portrayed herself to be a tough little thing and normally she would not shed a tear, at least in front of another person. I used to think she was fearless, but I was wrong.

There's a lot more to say about the paranormal activities at Squires Lane in 1971 to 72, before I do so, I think it would be appropriate to tell you that the "happenings" at the house were Poltergeist activity. My sister was the magnet for the Spirit or entity. I use the word entity because some people do not like to class a naughty or mischievous Spirit, as a Spirit at all. The word entity conjures up a much more detached image - more comfortable to deal with. Poltergeists usually function around people who are dysfunctional or going through puberty. The latter applied to her, but we didn't understand any of this at the time, so we felt that there was no choice but to live with it.

The "happenings" became more intense, more frightening. One morning she opened her eyes to find a man standing at the foot of the bed. As her brain became fully engaged, she realised that this person was not who she thought it was as he lived miles away and would never be in our house early in the morning. The realisation of this fact made her heart race as the fear rose inside her. As she stared into his eyes, they weren't the eyes of the man she knew; his were darker in colour. Everything else about his face, hair and clothes were the same. She suddenly felt rigid with fear, the figure disappeared in an instant and my sister did another one of those famous leaps out of bed and took flight downstairs.

Leading towards the Christmas of 1971, the situation became more intense. Our "nerves" were being eroded, we didn't understand what a Poltergeist was so it wasn't dealt with in the correct manner; we became more unnerved and unhappy, we just had to live with it. I clearly remember my thoughts that Christmas, I wondered how long it would all go on for, it felt never-ending. I felt the only way was to leave the house; I didn't, not until I was 22.

At the start of 1972 my brother seemed to be the target for the entity. One day he walked into his bedroom, to find a pair of his shoes shuffling around the floor. Danny said he didn't stay long enough to see if they were doing the waltz or the foxtrot! He was 15 at the time; he swore that not a drop of alcohol had passed his lips! This scared him half to death, from then until these events ceased, he slept in our bedroom with my younger sister and me. The event has scared him so much, that we eventually changed bedrooms permanently with him.

Danny has always seen spiritual and psychic phenomena, ever since he was small, but he doesn't like to discuss it. "Best forgotten," he says, this is because he is really scared. I may not be forgiven for talking about him in this book, however I have continued to do so because there are thousands of people like Danny; not sceptical, just afraid. What I mean is, that it is better to be open minded and afraid, than to "pull down the shutters" and try and ignore it and pretend it doesn't happen.

Over the months the entity seemed to get stronger. At first it was the feeling of a presence and noises, then objects being moved in front of our eyes. The whole fiasco reached a climax in February; mum walked into the bathroom to find the chrome shower attachment floating in mid air, high above the bath with its flexi-pipe trailing behind still attached to the bath. It took a couple of seconds for mum to make a move, she was frozen with shock at first then she slammed the door shut behind her, then went downstairs (I've just remembered Danny also witnessed this spectacle). She made a cup of tea, regained her composure and went back up to the bathroom. She found the shower attachment lying in the bath. As soon as I came in she told me about it, and it was clear to me the incident had scared her.

The worst incident for mum was the morning she walked into Danny's bedroom. She went in to wake him up with a cup of tea. What a frightening experience this was for her. All the bedding was on the floor, except for one sheet. This was over his body and had been meticulously tucked-in around him (I say *tucked-in* because it was so perfect it was impossible for him to have done it himself; mum said). The face was the scariest part, the sheet had been pressed into and around his features, and she said he looked like an Egyptian Mummy ready for burial. She was horrified; she told me there was a deathly feeling in the room. She lunged forward and grabbed the sheet, literally lifting it off Danny. Poor Danny, he was lying there in his underpants, he must have wondered what the hell was going on! Mum was shaking; this was the final straw! She told Danny that he had had the bedding tight over his face; she thought he might not have been able to breathe. Danny accepted her explanation for disturbing his precious sleep.

This was the point at which mum realised what was going on, there was a bad or evil presence in the house. She told me that the moment she ripped the sheet off Danny, she shouted, "Get out you bastard". This was instinct; she was protecting her child. She was the perfect person for the job. Now I'm older and wiser I have been able to talk to mediums and clergymen who've taken part in the freeing of earthbound Spirits or exorcisms. They have shared their knowledge with me and I am sure that mum did exactly the right thing; verbal brute force seems to be the key. The love mum had for her child gave her all the brute force she needed to succeed.

This was the end of the Poltergeist. We never knew who it was; I don't think I am bothered about knowing if I'm honest. The memories however did linger for a long time. The house was never the same again. Not just because of the Poltergeist, but the accumulation of all the other experiences that occurred there. My sister and I had a secret name for the house "Spooksville". It felt like that as far back as I can remember, right up to the last time I walked out through the door after the house had been sold following my dad's death. I just question "was it the house or was it the people in it that attracted all this unwanted paranormal activity?"

The family home in Squires Lane, Tyldesley, Lancashire.

Chapter Nineteen

Jenny

In 1984 I allowed myself to be persuaded into buying a puppy by my then husband. We already had one "little old man" called Pépé, a West Highland white terrier; to be honest I was reluctant as I thought one dog was enough. I lost my battle, and very reluctantly agreed to start the lengthy search round the country, for a breeder who had what we were looking for, a Dalmatian bitch puppy.

This wasn't an easy task, however, they do say, "good things don't come easy". Early in May we located a litter, the puppies were just three weeks old. On the phone, the breeder asked a lot of questions. Especially regarding our suitability to be good owners of one of her pups. Once we had passed the test, we were invited to go and see the litter; this journey took us to Staffordshire. The day was beautiful, bright and sunny, the puppies were adorable. Any major reservations I had had about buying a dog started to slip away as I held these "babies" in my arms.

It is often said the animals pick their owners not the other way around, in this case, that was certainly true. I had my eye on one pup, but another one climbed onto my lap and nestled down (I was sitting on the floor at the time). This was the start of a "love affair" between

"little Jenny" and me. The bonus was a very unusual friendship between "big Jenny" and myself, a friendship that was to last for ten years.

You have met Jenny in a couple of other chapters so now I will talk about her in much more depth, I hope that she will interest, entertain and amuse you, as she did me. She was a very busy lady when I met her, she ran a boarding kennel and cattery, a rescue for mistreated and abandoned animals plus she bred the occasional litter of Dalmatians. All this, as well as being a wife and mum, no mean feat in anyone's book. My memories of Jenny in the early years of our friendship were of a "whirlwind". On first meeting her, she told me that she did not have any time for a social life or friendships outside the home. So you will be able to imagine how taken aback I was when, a few weeks later after picking up my seven-week-old puppy, she rang and invited us over for tea. I was delighted, but a little puzzled, "why me?" she was breaking her rules, I couldn't help but wonder what had made her do that.

145

We did go for tea and it was a lovely, relaxed afternoon. I felt as though I had known her for years. Only months later did I ask her why she had broken her socialising/friendship rule. The answer she gave me was simply that she was "drawn to me". At the start of our relationship Jenny didn't know about my profession, I deliberately withheld the information from her, as I couldn't take the risk of her considering me "Too weird" to let me buy one of her precious puppies. She was delighted when the truth came out. She was also a firm believer in spiritual matters, and was no stranger to psychic and spiritual experiences. This was a simple case of "like attracting like".

From my point of view the friendship had got off to a good start, even before Jenny knew about me, she had made her mind up that she liked me and wanted my friendship. In my job it's easy to gather friends who want to know me for what I can do, not who I am.

At the end of our first visit, I was so pleased when she said, "will you come again?" I replied, "Yes please, I'd love to". A couple of weeks later Jenny rang with the invite and to make arrangements. To cut a long story short, this is when the secret of my profession was revealed. I wasn't available to take the call, so I rang her back. At that point I made my confession, she asked if I would do some work for her, I wholeheartedly agreed.

When I do my spiritual work, I like to sit down beforehand with pen and pad to "tune in". I then translate information that I receive from Spirits into words and write them down. Then at the arranged time, I read these back to my client and this is the basis of the sitting. To the layperson it may sound silly or unbelievable, but this is how I work and it's comfortable for me. During the second journey to see Jenny and her family, I made my notes in the car travelling down the motorway (I wasn't driving). We arrived at her home and after settling in, I showed her the notes I had made. She was amazed, but she couldn't get her head around how this was possible. I told her not to even try; even other mediums have asked me in the past, how I was able to work for people without them being present.

During the ten years that we were "earth friends", Jenny became an accomplished writer, many of her articles, ranging from fact to fantasy, including love stories, were published in a range of magazines. This multitalented woman later wrote a monthly column in a kennel magazine and a novel, which she didn't manage to get published during her lifetime. She even wrote an article about me, which was published in "Woman's World" magazine in June 1990 entitled "There's a happy medium".

As you can gather, my friend was an extremely versatile person. Most people who met her felt she was quite extraordinary. She loved a challenge and didn't like to be beaten by anything. The one and only thing that did get the better of her was agoraphobia. She was already a sufferer when I met her. It had started when Samantha, her daughter, was quite small. She told me it started in a very small way, and then grew until it consumed her. At first, she put on her "boxing gloves" and tried to do battle with it. Trying every therapy that was available at the time, but eventually admitted defeat. She told me "this is about accepting what you have got, not worrying about what you haven't". This woman had a personality, which was larger than life; she took all her skills and talents and made a very good life for herself, within the confines of her home and land.

In 1997 the kennel was sold and the family moved to a smallholding on a hill at the other side of the valley. Right from the start this house became a hive of activity, for a few years the writing dominated her world, along with caring for animals. Then came hand-painted clothing, for the family craft-fair business. Sometimes she made me dizzy just watching her. I envied her energy and motivation.

You may think I am talking about "Superwoman"; she did portray this image. I was one of only a few people who were lucky enough to be close to her and even though, like all of us, she had a vulnerable side, she was the nearest person I have ever met to being a "Superwoman". There was a very special aspect to our friendship, a spiritual/psychic inter-linking. I consider myself very lucky. What I'm talking about is a spontaneous connection made between two people at a time of anxiety, pain or even joy. I know there will be many of you saying "I have one of those", it's a wonderful thing to have, so treasure it and know it's special.

The first time this link revealed itself was in 1989; I had been feeling unwell for some time, on one particular afternoon, I began to feel very "strange". Suddenly, two of the fingers on my right hand went completely numb; there was no feeling in them. They were ice-cold to the touch and I couldn't move them. Unbeknown to me at that time, I was having a panic attack; it really was quite scary. Because I didn't understand what was happening I became tearful. Just then, the phone rang; it was Jenny "is there something wrong?" She asked. I was very surprised to hear her voice; I burst into tears and told her what was happening. She talked to me, which helped to calm me down. Then she explained that she had been busy with the animals and suddenly my face came into her mind, this was accompanied by an uneasy feeling so she rang me straight away. I know the situation wasn't serious, but it was a great comfort to know that there was one person, out in the world, who was psychically linked with me. This was the first of many such phone-calls we made to each other at a time of need. Apart from these conscious connections, we both experienced "dreams" containing a direct message or prediction for each other. There always seemed to be an urgency to relay the contents of the dream to the other person, after we had spoken, it felt for me as though a weight was lifted from my shoulders.

Regardless of our psychic connections, I would never have called us "soul-mates" because we were very different people. We had a number of opinions on things about which we agreed to differ. She was a strong willed, stubborn "so-and-so", but when it came down to the things that really matter, the spiritual beliefs that were the core of our friendship, these over-rode our differences. Such friendships are rare and should be treasured.

Just before Christmas in 1988, I received a very strange phone call from my friend. At first she was chatting away quite normally, then she made a very profound statement, she said to me "no matter what happens in life, I shall always be in contact with you, we shall always be friends". The statement was out of context to the rest of the conversation. For some reason, I didn't reply. I was very used to her making statements of all kinds, they were usually very useful to me sooner or later, and so I took it and stored it away in my mind. It was almost seven years before I really understood what she had meant; this was after her sudden passing in August 1995, was this a case of "unconscious knowing"?

For many years Jenny saw animal Spirits, as well as people. The animal appearances were almost daily; in fact they used to run her ragged. She often told me about "falling over a dog that wasn't there!" Then one day the ultimate wild goose chase came. She was in her hall when suddenly a Dalmatian (or so she thought) rushed past her and nearly knocked her flying, it went out of the door and into the field. Her first thoughts were that the dog might escape off her land and onto the road. She ran like crazy, when she reached the far corner of the field and she realised there was no dog to be seen; it had actually vanished into thin air. It was at this point that she realised she had been had, on returning to the house she found the dog that she thought she was chasing, relaxing on the couch in the lounge!

When Jenny phoned me to tell me about this incident, we fell about with laughter, but not all of her spiritual experiences were so amusing. Before I move onto more "heavy stuff", I want to tell you about a happening that occurred while she was living at the kennel on Biddulph Moor, Staffordshire. It was a lovely summer afternoon; as usual she was up to her elbows in muck (literally). She just happened to look up from doing her task, when she saw a man, heading towards the door of the farmhouse. Muttering a few choice words to herself, she ran towards him. Before she had a chance to shout, he had stepped inside the house. Visitors were supposed to wait at the side gate and ring the bell, so she wasn't too happy with this man.

From the moment she first saw him, until the moment she stepped inside the house, she never took her eyes off him. Consequently, she was a little more than shocked when she found the house empty. Her comment to me at that time was "they've got me jumping through bloody hoops". I've never met anyone who has been given the run around by the Spirits as much as Jenny, as I hope these two incidents demonstrate.

I believe one of the symptoms of agoraphobia is the dread of the being trapped in an enclosed space. The fact that Jenny never left her home ground made her feel that this could never happen to her as she felt fully in control of her environment. Then one day, she just started getting feelings of "being shut in a room"; the door just wouldn't open. She was sure that this was a premonition. It made her cautious, she started to leave the door open when she went into a room on her own, her logic was that if it wasn't fastened, then it couldn't get stuck. These feelings came and went, as did her exercising caution, but of course the dreaded day did arrive. This day she was making a fire in the lounge, when she came to leave the room, the door just would not open.

Jenny became hysterical, after doing everything she could think of to try to open it, she began shouting and screaming. Unfortunately all of this fell on stony ground, there was no one else in the house to hear or help. Some time passed and she calmed down a little, then she tried the door again. This time it just opened, the handle wasn't broken or sticking. It was very clear to Jenny that this was spiritually motivated, what she couldn't understand was why?

When she asked me what it was all about, I was unable to help. The only explanation I could offer was that I thought the Spirits were trying to tell her something, something only she would understand. After this event the waves of fear at being locked in a room just stopped. Slowly, over the following weeks, Jenny started to relax. A few months later, she was alone in the house when she heard the sound of water running fiercely in the bathroom. Immediately she ran upstairs to find water splashing everywhere, the cold tap had been turned fully on. She reached for the tap and as she did so, the door slammed shut behind her. She twisted and pulled at the handle, she was out of her mind with panic and fear. Miraculously she managed to gain a level head by stepping back for a moment. She then tried the door again, this time it just opened. There were a few incidents of this kind that took place in the bathroom over a period of about three years.

So what was it all about? Why did the Spirits have to create situations that would scare this lady half to death? She was a firm believer; she didn't need dramatic experiences to convince her of anything. The answer for her, and for any of us, is that we are not listening to what the Spirits are telling us. I believe that they always start off with a more gentle approach. Then if we don't take notice, usually because we are too busy getting on with our lives, they move on to more drastic measures. I speak from personal experience here; I'm very guilty of ignoring warnings in the past, so I have had to be shaken in order for me to take notice.

It is only in retrospect that I know that the Spirits were trying to warn Jenny about her health. She was a very strong-minded person, if I had "known" that her health was at risk due to the hectic lifestyle and had proceeded with advice, such as "take it easy", she would not have thanked me for it. I feel that the Spirits were dealing with her first hand, they clearly didn't get their messages across; or did they? Knowing this lady as I did, no one told her what to do not even the Spirits. The more time passes since her death, the surer I become that she knew there was a serious problem. We are all creatures with free will; Jenny chose to look the other way. The Spirits never told me that she had a weakness within her heart. I thank God for that, I could never have told her. This is a classic example of not mixing mediumship with friendship.

Every year I would visit Jenny over the Christmas period, as a sort of gift I was usually able to give her a few assorted messages about the year ahead. She didn't ask it was something I liked to do for my friend. At Christmas 1994, I had only one message; we stood in the hallway admiring her beautiful decorations, I said to her, "Well Jenny, next year is the year that changes everything for us". Her response was very serious, she said, "Shut up, you're scaring me". How correct I was, on the 30th August Jenny collapsed in the bathroom during the night and passed over very quickly due to a heart problem. In April of that year I met Martin, we became friends and I left an unhappy marriage in the November and moved to the south of England with him.

Jenny always liked me to be honest with her if I was giving her any messages or spiritual advice. In the 1980s Barry (Jenny's husband) suffered a collapsed lung for the second time. He was very poorly and was rushed to hospital for surgery. On the day of the operation, I had a very vivid clairvoyant picture, which ran like the movie. I saw a hearse turning around at the top of their drive. The sun was shining; it was a clear day although there was a slight chill in the air. The only sound I could hear was that of the hearse's tyres crunching the gravel. I was also aware of my being an observer of the scene.

Once I knew that Barry was recovering from the surgery, I phoned Jenny. I told her that I had seen something very serious and asked her if she wanted to know about it. She said "yes"; so I went on to describe my clairvoyant vision. Between us we decided that, Barry must have been very sick, much worse than anyone knew, and this was a forewarning of what might happen. I know she never told Barry (to my knowledge); in fact we never spoke about it again.

On the sixth of September 1995, I sat in a parked car, at the bottom of Jenny's drive. I watched from a distance as the hearse carrying my friend Jenny's coffin slowly turned around crunching the gravel on the driveway. The sun was shining and there was a slight chill in the air. My clairvoyant picture had shown me her funeral, not Barry's. I'm so glad that I hadn't understood what the Spirits had shown me. I had thought that it was a wasted exercise when Barry made a good recovery (sorry to sound so disappointed Barry). My learning here was that the message was for me, not for Jenny, maybe time for me to prepare for the physical loss of a good friend; only I hadn't realised what they were telling me!

The day before my friend passed to Spirit, Tuesday 29 August, started off as a very ordinary day. Work in the morning followed by a lovely walk in the fields with my sister. At about four o'clock in the afternoon, we were drinking tea when I suddenly developed a headache, not unusual for me but this was accompanied by a deep strong pain in my chest. At first I thought it was physical, so I took 2 Paracetamol. The pain continued to bore away at me until 9 o'clock in the evening. It was at this stage that I realised that the pain was a psychic connection, rather than physical. My dad often lets me know he's around by giving me a "quick stab in the heart", I relate to this because of the terrible heart attack he suffered before he passed. This was different, but I didn't understand.

The following morning I awoke at 7.30. Barry phoned me at 8.30, he just said "Jenny's dead". The moment I received Barry's phone call, the whole thing fitted together like a jigsaw. The results of the post-mortem revealed a split in the aorta about an inch above her heart. This was the same place where I had experienced the pain. For some time I experienced a lot of guilt. Was this Jenny reaching out to me psychically for help? Could I have done anything to help if I had realised what was happening? I don't have answers to these questions at this time, I don't know if I ever will.

Since her passing I have had only four spiritual experiences regarding Jenny. Two have been "dreams" which I believe to be astral meetings. In neither did she speak, but we were very "together". In the second one she put her arms around me, something she would never have done on earth. On two occasions I have felt her sitting on the side of my bed. One occurred the night before my driving test, but the more intense experience took place a few days prior to my leaving my ex-husband in 1995. She arrived at about midnight and stayed with me all night. I woke a few times and was surprised to feel her still sitting there. She stayed until the morning. Our friendship lives on as she promised it would!

I hope you enjoy this poem given to me by Jenny; it was one of the many she wrote.

Time Again

Could we but have our time again,
To saunter gently down the lane,
And look with wonder, hope and peace,
Upon the green and merry trees,
To see again the rose hip hue,
And gaze transfixed upon the view,
Of summertime in gold and green,
Often looked at, never seen,
To watch again the butterfly,
Who arches skyward as we lie,
Within the clover, heady, sweet,
Purple, white, painter's feast,
To watch the rooks high in the elm,
Cloistered, peaced, rooky realm,
To smell again the daisy dew,
To have again the self that's you,
Could we but have our time again,
Before the winter, fore the pain,
Before the snow could wash us clean,
When summertime was summer's dream.

Jennifer G. Jones

Jenny and me cuddling animals and putting the world to rights.

Chapter Twenty

Mediumship in Children

When you were a child, did you have any "imaginary friends?" Many children do because children do see Spirits. Children often see Spirit children rather than Spirit adults; I guess that is because they are less likely to be afraid of one of their peers. What they see is real, yet they instinctively know there is something different or special about their "visitor". It is the adults that insist that these children are imaginary because many, thank god not all, do find the prospect of their child seeing a Spirit daunting, frightening or quite simply socially unacceptable. By telling a child they can't really see a "friend" the child will become so confused that it will "Close its mind", this will, more than likely, end the magical period of time where seeing Spirits is a natural occurrence in life. I think many grown-ups have much to answer for, don't you?

I believe we're all born with a sixth sense. It is stronger within some people than in others. More people remember seeing Spirits when they were small, up to about eight years old, than at any other time in their lives. Of course the type of environment we are brought up in will either make or break the natural development of the sixth sense. In the "spiritually/ psychically friendly" household it is very likely that children will develop into highly intuitive adults. If the household has a suppressed attitude to these matters then the children will be more likely just to develop a normal amount of instinct. In a way I'm an exception to the rule, we were extremely spiritually suppressed as a family and I now do this job. What happened to me was, it was driven down but not out and it all re-emerged at a suitable time when I was older and living away from the family home.

I was once told about a young girl who was incredibly psychic and spiritually aware. She saw Spirits on a regular basis, but she was also clairvoyant, she could "see" very accurately world events and was quite open with her predictions. Her parents were very well known figures in the local community. He father was a professional person and her mother was a member of every guild and charity in the area. They decided that they could not have this "embarrassment", they thought of their daughter as a freak, so they made the decision to "knock it on the head". They smacked her, threatened her and even locked her in her room and withdrew privileges in an attempt to do so.

How very cruel and very ignorant these people were! It seemed that they only cared about their position and social standing. When their daughter was old enough, she left home. She was a bright, intelligent girl who had the world at her feet. She possessed these marvellous "gifts". After years of struggling, she met a man and fell in love. This man gave his permission (I think permission is a good word here) to be herself. Her spiritual gift developed, she became a healer, all this happened because she was loved and supported. I wonder how her parents coped with the shame of their daughter walking out on them, was that more socially acceptable than having a medium and healer in the family? It isn't my place to judge or comment, but I have to say that I have met a lot of people like these through the years and I feel a great sense of pity for people who function with such a small and closed-minded attitude.

Because of the spiritually stifled attitude that my brother, sisters and I were brought up in, my sister decided when my nephew Jonathan was born in 1984 that if ever her son showed any psychic tendencies as he grew up, she would do her best to nurture the situation. Even when he was a small child his parents realised that Jonathan was spiritually aware. He was a regular recipient of nocturnal visitors. On many occasions he was found standing up in his cot deep in "conversation" with a "visitor", the rest of the household wasn't very happy about this as Jonathan would often end up in tears, he was tired and his Spirit friend obviously wanted to play.

The early Spirit visitors were just the start of a series of Spirit encounters that this young man would experience over the next few years. I will tell you more as we progress. What happened in my nephew's bedroom was by no means unique, many people witness such scenes and choose to dismiss them or simply say no more about them. One of my main reasons for writing this book is to encourage people to think more and say more about unusual happenings. There is a great fear of ridicule from the sceptics which makes people reluctant to speak out and that is so sad as the world is full of untold stories.

You met Elsie in an earlier chapter about suicide; I mentioned she was quite a character. It came as no surprise to me that the baby she gave birth to when she was 45 (a great shock to her and her husband although extremely welcome in the family) started to grow up to be very psychic and extremely spiritually aware. Elsie told me that as soon as Diane was born, she knew she was special; she behaved differently to Elsie's other children, and from the many children that had grown-up around her belonging to other family members and friends. Elsie told me it was very difficult to explain, in many ways she was like other little girls, however things did develop and it became very clear that Diane was interacting with Spirits. By the time she was 3, she would give Elsie detailed accounts of the Spirit visitors that she had had. One day she described perfectly a lady and the clothes that she was wearing. This was Elsie's grandmother, Diane's great grandmother, who had been in the Spirit world for many years, the little girl didn't know that she'd ever existed.

Elsie hastily dug out an old photograph of this lady and showed it to Diane with the question "Is this the lady you saw?" She replied "yes" then she went on to tell Elsie what the lady had said to her, detail which escapes me now but which was very accurate and meant a lot to her. I did ask Elsie if there had been a chance that Diane could have seen the photograph at an earlier date and used her memory to create the situation. She told me that the photo was in a box on top of the wardrobe, which hadn't been lifted down since Diane was born. I always like to check these things out because if we don't then the sceptics will! For me this was a genuine case of mediumship in children.

The next example involves my nephew Jonathan and me back in 1986 when he was just two years old. I had just had a week's holiday in Worcestershire, at which time I discovered I was pregnant. It was unplanned, so I was very shocked, upon my return from the holiday I went to see my younger sister to discuss the situation with her. We talked quite openly whilst she bathed Jonathan, not thinking for one moment that he was listening to our conversation, let alone understanding it. Well, I was very wrong, once he was dressed in his pyjamas and his mum had gone to prepare his supper, he walked over to me, put his hand on my arm and said "no baby" then off he toddled to search out his supper. That was on Saturday evening 14th June 1996, on the Wednesday my baby was miscarried at home.

I can't remember Jonathan giving me a message as significant as that ever again, nevertheless he had a number of experiences, which he never hesitated to share with those around him. When he was about 8 years old, early one morning he was playing in the cloakroom area under the stairs situated in his dining room. He saw just the hand of a small child, reaching out to him. He was so shocked and frightened that he shot out of the area like a bullet from a gun! He was left pale faced and speechless, after he had calmed down he was able to describe in more detail exactly what he had seen. The description he gave was of a small hand with fingers outstretched reaching out, trying to touch him. There was no arm attached; yet he knew instinctively that it was a boy and he gave his age (this unfortunately escapes me)

His mother was able to tie these details into some facts. The age of this Spirit child coincided with the time that had elapsed since she had miscarried a baby very early in pregnancy. She had been taking some particular tablets, which were withdrawn from the market because there was evidence that they could cause damage to unborn babies. The miscarriage had been nature's way of preventing a lifetime of suffering for this person. She came to the conclusion that this Spirit was Jonathan's brother who had come to play. This was not the first time this Spirit child had made an appearance. A few years earlier Jonathan's dad had bumped into him on the landing one night, as he got up to go to the bathroom. Bleary eyed he thought at first it was

Jonathan, he bent down in an attempt to guide him back to bed, as he did the "boy" just disappeared. He soon realised it wasn't Jonathan!!

In February 1988 there was a very sad loss in the family, Candy a beautiful golden retriever died very suddenly, she collapsed on a walk and had to be rushed off to the emergency vet's who's tests revealed her heart had developed cancer. She was peacefully put to sleep and my sister and brother-in-law brought her body home. I had safely  tucked Jonathan up in bed so he was unaware of the events of that evening. When he got up on the Sunday morning, the news was broken to him; he was clearly upset by this and went to play quietly in the lounge. As a four-year-old he had already encountered death within the family on more than one occasion, he had asked questions such as "where have they gone?" So he was already forming a basic understanding that the Spirit lives in the body and when the body dies the Spirit goes to "Heaven".

Some time passed and Jonathan emerged from the lounge, he told his mum that "Dee Dee" (Candy's pet name) had been playing with him on the rug. Unprompted he said that she had looked like a puppy and that she didn't have sore legs anymore. His mother was very pleased by this even though she was feeling a deep sense of grief, then she said, "what happened next?" To which he replied, "then the magic was gone"

I think this demonstrates for us that even a four-year-old has the ability to recognise when something is "unearthly" and what an innocent, yet perfect, choice of the word "magic". Anyone who has seen a Spirit will tell you that there is something so different and so special about the experience, which truly is "magical".

I find it very sad, that we have so many natural mediums in our midst that are "cut down" in their prime by the adult world. No wonder children and young people become so confused, they are so often stopped from doing what comes naturally.

Chapter Twenty-One

Peter and John

A friend of mine once asked me "why do people come to see you?" The only answer I could give was "anything and everything". Because that is true, no reason is too trivial or too obscure to seek advice or help about. When I was a teenager I watched an American film with my dad, it was a film about a very rich man who, before he died, he videoed himself reading his last will and testament. After his death, the video was played to the family. This was full of surprises, apart from most of the family not getting what they were expecting. He also told each one of them exactly what he thought of them, both the good and bad stuff.

My dad loved it; he told me that he would love to do that (he never did) it was both amusing and shocking. I felt it could be a very good idea, ensuring that no one would be in any doubt about the wishes of the deceased. I never imagined, at that time, that in the future I would come across a real life situation, which was of a similar nature. During the early years of my career, a gentleman called Peter came to see me for a sitting. He lived and worked in the south of England. Occasionally his work as a chauffeur brought him to the north and that was how he found me. I've never forgotten this man or this sitting because it was one of the most unusual ones I have ever done. He was a very troubled person; luckily within a short time of the sitting starting I "hit the spot". A Spirit called John joined us; he introduced himself to me very clearly. I passed this on to Peter, who looked at me with disbelief. I asked him what was wrong, he said, "I'll tell you when you have told me what he has to say". I continued, passing John's apologies to Peter, I didn't know what he was referring to. There was a little more dialogue; I just did my job passing it on from John to Peter. I felt totally in the dark, but that's nothing new!

Peter didn't keep me in the dark for long. I had done my job and he was satisfied. He took an envelope from his pocket; he opened it to reveal some Polaroid photographs of a naked lady. I have to say I was very shocked at first, I just didn't understand the relevance of them, soon Peter explained. John, the Spirit who had communicated with us, had left these photographs with a solicitor. It was his wish, expressed in his will that they be given to Peter after his death. These photos were of Peter's wife; they had been married for about three years at the time of John's death. There was also a letter of explanation for Peter. Since his wife had been a very young woman, her mother had encouraged her four brothers (one of whom was John) to use her, their niece, for sexual gratification. She had been sterilised as a teenager (illegally), which had left her badly scarred. His wife told Peter that she had undergone major surgery in her youth, which had left her unable to have children. Peter came to see me before he had confronted his wife with the photographs and letter. The part he was finding too difficult to handle was the fact that throughout their marriage, she had made periodic visits to the country to visit the remaining uncles, always alone, obviously doing her "duty".

At this point in the sitting I asked John why he had done such a thing to Peter, he told me, he had done it because he was jealous of him, he didn't want to share his wife. Peter did not accept the apology; he could not forgive John for leaving him such a legacy. It was very clear that John wanted to cause Peter a great deal of emotional pain, he certainly succeeded, he also destroyed the marriage from the other side of the grave.

I asked Peter if he would be able to forgive his wife, he said, "no I can't". I did point out to him that his wife had always obeyed instructions from her mother and, even though this woman had died a number of years earlier, his wife was programmed to do exactly as her mother had told her to do, and what these men expected of her. In my mind she was not a bad person. Peter told me he felt used and humiliated, he could not go on living with a person that he could not trust. I asked, "what if John had not left the photos and the letter?" He replied, "well, I may never have known and everything would have carried on the same". John had clearly shattered his world, Peter said "this man was either very cruel or he had a twisted, strange sense of humour!" I had to agree. The apology made by John from the Spirit world to Peter on earth was not accepted, I sensed an element of regret in John's voice; but it was all too late.

We talked in great depth about the situation. Mediumship wasn't instrumental in the discovery of the situation, however it did build a bridge between the two men. After the sitting I thought a lot about it, I reflected on other situations in the past when a Spirit has had "an axe to grind ". Some Spirits can be very outspoken, even hurtful. I've been told about some very unusual requests that people have specified in their wills but this one "takes the biscuit!"

Wouldn't it be wonderful if people could sort things out as they move through their lives! If they need to speak out, they should do so. Relationships seem to be the worst affected area, we can't remain friends with everyone we know for life, but where people really matter and communication has broken down, why do we leave it all hanging by a thread? There's always the answer or excuse, I'll sort it next week, or tomorrow, or whenever, but for some people tomorrow never comes. Lots of people pass to Spirit with a lifetime of frustration, resentment and regret. They take these feelings with them to the Spirit world, a mass of unfinished business.

The case of John and Peter has taught me a lot. It's no use thinking that you'll be able to make everything all right from the other side of the grave, being "dead" doesn't earn one the right to automatic forgiveness from the living.

Chapter Twenty-Two

Lisa

Quite often in my career I have been involved with what feels like, whole families, three or four members of the same family would come to see me to seek help or advice on individual or family issues. Earlier in the book you met Susan, the lady who saw the feathery object float down to the table during a sitting. Her son Neil first came to see me when he was a teenager in the army, then there was a gap of seven or eight years before he made a return visit. I was delighted that he had approached me for help, although the reasons for his return were extremely sad.

He made this visit early in 1995, just a few weeks after his wife Lisa, aged 26 years had passed to Spirit after suffering a brain haemorrhage. Even though I never physically met her, through doing this and a further sitting a few months later, I felt very close to her, she was a marvellous Spirit to work with, she made my job a real pleasure to do.

In life Lisa was a bright and lively character, full of fun. She had an intelligent mind and a creative personality. It was, according to Neil, a terrible loss to a lot of people, not just the immediate family. "Everybody loved Lisa," he told me. She was mum to 4 small children and absolutely adored by Neil. My main reason for telling Lisa's story is to demonstrate the power of spiritual love and to explain how faith, belief and love can transcend two planes. Contrary to the belief of many "Experts" in fields such as Psychology and Psychiatry, mediumship can aid rather than hinder the grieving process.

Neil came from a family who had strong spiritual beliefs. Lisa was also a spiritualist; her contact with Neil after her death helped him to heal and to be able to carry on with his life and to personally care for their children. This is what she would have wanted or even expected him to do, she did all that was in her power to help him achieve this major task.

Neil told me that Lisa had been suffering with headaches for about two years. The doctor had not ordered any tests; he just gave her painkillers. She wasn't really satisfied but she did what most people do, she carried on taking the tablets. It is quite common for people to do odd or unexpected things shortly before they pass to Spirit. (I put this down to subconscious knowing). Lisa was no exception; about two weeks before her death she asked Neil to sort out some life insurance on her. To cut a long story short, he said he would, but he didn't - time simply ran out! On the day that Lisa suffered the brain haemorrhage, she had visited the hairdresser, Neil told me that she always looked nice to him but on the day she passed away, she looked exceptionally lovely. The haemorrhage occurred in her sleep and she never woke again. When Neil realised something was very wrong she

165

was rushed to hospital and put on life support. Tests showed she was brain dead and the machine was switched off.

Only people who have experienced such a situation, can Imagine the pain and confusion that Neil was feeling on that day. When he came to me for his first sitting he described the first 24 hours after Lisa's death as being like "the end of the world". He felt he didn't have the strength or motivation to carry on without her. "So what changed?" I enquired. Within a very short time he could hear Lisa's voice, very clearly inside his head, she was giving him encouragement to carry on, with some directions. She was always a great organiser both of people and getting things done. He told me "the words seemed to penetrate the grief I was feeling". He went on to say that it felt as though he was being "Shaken out of shock". Very soon he could feel her presence in the house, there were smells that had been unique to her and he experienced an increasing feeling of closeness. All this happened before the funeral, so it made a dreadfully difficult ordeal, much more tolerable.

Things started to happen with great regularity after the funeral, he started to see mists and wispy images around the house. The smells, or maybe I should describe them as fragrances, increased. This feeling of being "organised" from above was probably the most reassuring of the experiences. Neil told me there were certain people who had judged him for healing too quickly. They said the speed, at which he had recovered and regained a sense of normality in his life, after just a few weeks, had offended a number of people; they thought this disrespectful to Lisa. People either closed their minds to his words or refused to understand that he and Lisa were still a team, working as one in an attempt to keep the family together and the household running smoothly as it always had.

Yes, there was no doubt he was doing very well, but he did feel the emotional pain of her physical loss and there were some very black days, hitting "rock bottom" never lasted long, she would often draw close and help lift him up from the depths. Neil told me that he had found it unbelievable that people expected him to live in a "pit" and to stay there until a respectable period of time had passed, a very Victorian attitude he thought. Very sadly he did lose friends and the support of some family members because of this, but he had to do what he felt natural and be true to himself and Lisa.

Between his first and second visit to see me in 1995, Neil had what was for him the "ultimate experience". One evening he was sitting on the settee when something caught his attention. He saw movement out of the corner of his eye, on turning round he saw Lisa, just the top part of her body had materialised. The experience was quite brief but very clear, he told me it made his heart flutter and he went hot under the collar. At the time this occurred Neil was making some personal decisions relating to change, he felt it was so relevant that she should appear at that time, he felt supported by her in his decision-making.

Lisa's visit prompted Neil to ring me and make an appointment for a further sitting. I too felt the timing was good because the sitting was an "absolute cracker" in my opinion. Before we had time to exchange pleasantries, things got underway. I could feel Lisa in the room and she started talking to me about things that were happening for Neil. I passed these details on and Neil confirmed that they were correct. As usual Lisa did have a lot to say and Neil was delighted. She really was a chatterbox. Most of the messages were verbal, delivered at the speed of an "express train". She was exceptionally good at communication especially taking into account the fact that she was a new Spirit. She was also very good at making the temperature in the room change, which was quite dramatic. One moment it was warm the next it was rather chilly, giving us tingles and "goose flesh". It almost felt that she was playing games with us, and then the nicest thing happened. Between us, there was a strange feeling, I couldn't see her but I could feel a sensation, a mass of psychic energy near my knee. I was able to describe a female kneeling down between us; I sensed she was resting her hands on her thighs. Neil was delighted, "this is how she used to sit at the side of me; she hardly ever sat on the couch as she liked to be on the floor".

Next I got an urge to reach forward with my hand, I was able to feel the "mass" that was Lisa's spiritual body. I invited Neil to reach out and touch her, he did and he became quite emotional. The experience was fantastic, emotionally empowering. From a professional point of view, I felt privileged to be a part of this intimate reunion, from a personal point of view, I had all my spiritual beliefs reinforced in a few moments.

Lisa was her usual practical self that day, she told Neil it was time to sort out the remainder of her personal belongings. She insisted that everything should be put to good use. Clothes should go to friends and charity, however, before he did that she wanted him to make up four boxes for the children. Each box was to have a selection of her personal belongings in it, plus an item of clothing, she also said she would guide him in his selection. The boxes were to be kept safe until the children were old enough to appreciate the value their contents. This sitting really was magic, it was such a delight for me and we both shed tears of joy.

Neil took great pleasure at this second meeting to share with me the details of a "dream" he had recently had. I use the word dream with great reservation, as I believe he was in a "dream state", what he experienced was a spiritual/astral meeting with Lisa. In the "dream" he was hand-in-hand with her. She looked marvellous. Gently she led him and showed him the place to which she had been taken when she first passed over. (The "meeting" took place a few months after her passing). Firstly, they walked into a room that looked like a ward with beds on either side; it looked more like a dormitory than a hospital ward. In the beds there were people who looked sick, most of whom were sleeping. Next, they passed through some doors into another room. The people in there were sitting up in bed, they looked brighter, and they were chatting and laughing amongst themselves. Some of the people were old, others young. One was black, and in general it was clear to see that people were of various nationalities. In here the feeling or vibration was much lighter. Then, through even more doors into a third room, this was wonderful. Still there were beds, however in here people were walking around and sitting in chairs. People looked well and physically complete, no one was disabled or showed signs of physical injury. One thing that was outstanding was that the older people didn't have an "aged look" as if all the troubles of life, which would have been etched on their faces, had fallen away. The feeling in this room was one of overwhelming peace and calm.

It was at this final stage of the journey that Lisa turned to Neil and kissed him. The next thing he knew was waking up in his own bed. He told me he felt very strange, as if he had been "somewhere". Then it took quite a time for him to adjust to his earthly surroundings. Lisa was very clear in his mind; he could still feel her hand in his and the kiss on his lips. The part, which was most outstanding, was the fact that she didn't speak one word to him in the "dream", they had communicated with their minds. He told me, "verbal communication doesn't exist in the spiritual world, people speak with their hearts and minds and everything is so real and genuine".

It is my belief that Neil had been on an astral journey to the Spirit world. We will talk more about astral journeys in the next chapter. Whilst I have been writing the account of Neil's experiences I felt as though I was writing fantasy, almost too good to be true! But I was reminded, as I wrote, of the similarity between this and those accounts given to me by other people. I just have to make a comment and say, "everyone can't be wrong!"

The first draft of this chapter was written in September 1997. The week when it felt as though the whole nation has been stopped in its tracks by the death of Diana, Princess of Wales. Hundreds of thousands of people were making their pilgrimage to London to write personal messages in one of the books of condolence at Saint James's Palace. I understand those feelings of uselessness when grief strikes; this was their way of doing something, being useful in some way. Whilst I was writing about Lisa and Neil's tour of the place that awaits new Spirits when they enter the Spirit world, I had the reassurance that no matter what position you hold in this life, whether you are a princess or a wife and mother like Lisa, we are all going to the same place. When one passes over very suddenly like Diana, through the car crash, or Lisa, through her brain haemorrhage, it is such a shock for the Spirit to be catapulted from this world to the next without warning; no wonder Spirits need time to recover from their transition and then to come to terms with their new world.

So vivid was Neil's "dream" that he brought me a sketch of the wards and the people. I haven't included it in the book because I am sure that you, the reader, will have no difficulty in visualizing this for yourself.

Chapter Twenty-Three

Astral Travel

Astral travel is a term that describes a whole range of experiences. Many people experience it whilst in a "dream state"; others are able to induce it at will. It is one of those spiritual experiences that can leave a person questioning, "did I or didn't I?" When it is experienced in a "dream state" the memory of it lingers, it often has a three-dimensional aspect to it, not flat like a normal dream.

What is astral travel? I like to describe it as, the Spirit taking flight rather than breaking free. When the Spirit does "break free" this means you are "dead"! The spiritual body is attached to the physical body with a "silver cord" when it takes flights, no matter how far the distance it may travel from the physical body, the person will continue to breathe and function, so it is something that we need not fear.

The people, who make these journeys at will, usually do so by firstly becoming very relaxed to a stage where the body offers no resistance when the Spirit leaves the body. I have already mentioned that I'm a coward so I haven't mastered this technique yet. I do have a great desire to help other people achieve this experience, and then maybe I'll have the confidence to follow.

I have however, experienced many astral journeys during my sleep state and I confess that they are wonderful. There's nothing to fear, an astral journey is very different from a near death experience. The journey can be a trip to the future or the past and occasionally the present, often to another part of the country or even the world. A near death experience is something that happens to those people who "brush" with death or indeed die and are revived. Most people read about these in magazines and books, many have been lucky enough to experience it or have met someone who has had this experience. In the course of my job and in my everyday life, I have spoken to people who, whilst in a dramatic situation, have had a near death experience.

Each account is very individual, yet they all link together due to certain ingredients being present in their stories, a bright light, a feeling of being in a tunnel and the vision of one or a number of people, often familiar faces, saying words such as "it's not your turn" or "go back". As I write I'm aware that this may sound a little "corny". But please believe me, when a person who has experienced such an event relays it to you and you can witness the emotion in their eyes and hear it in the voice, there's nothing "corny" or unbelievable about it. The most common factor in these accounts has been the feeling of disappointment at having to return to their earthly body and the overwhelming feelings of love and peace that they encountered were fantastic.

Before I move on to examples I want to say that we are dealing with a variety of experiences here: -

Astral travel, journeys through time or over great distance.

Astral journeys to the Spirit world.

Near death experience.

Out of body experience.

The latter is the most simple to deal with; quite often the Spirit simply pops out, then pops back into the body. One client told me that she could float at will to the corner of the room and see herself lying in bed. The most common accounts relate to people seeing themselves undergoing surgery or at the scene of an accident. I like to describe this as the Spirit taking stock of the situation at that moment.

I thought about different accounts that have been given to me over the years and, whilst doing so, my driving instructor's account came to mind. I must admit that I was taken by surprise when, near the end of a lesson Barry, a rather wacky individual with a great sense of humour, started to tell me about something that had happened to him when he was 16. He had become very ill, suffering from pneumonia, he remembered the incident very clearly even though it was 40 years ago. He recalled the doctor making a visit; he was so weak that the doctor had to put his arm under his head in order to raise it off the pillow. In those days the medication was not as effective as it is today, so the situation was "touch and go" for a few days.

Whilst he was so ill, Barry had an amazing experience that has stayed with him ever since. He slipped into a deep sleep and then "awoke" to find himself in a dark tunnel; he was upright and moving forward slowly down the tunnel. The action was a "glide" rather than a "float". He felt in control of the movement, it certainly didn't feel against his will. At the bottom of the tunnel was an extremely bright light; it was small and round and blindingly bright. As Barry moved nearer, the light became larger and brighter. The feelings that dominated him were those of an overwhelming desire to move to the light. He also felt cocooned with peace and serenity, something he had never experienced before. I asked him what his thoughts were at that moment and he replied "no fear or hesitation, just a feeling of wanting to reach out to the light".

The next thing he remembered was waking up. His head was full of the memory of the journey. I asked him if he thought this had simply been a dream but he told me "definitely not". He had been very ill for days but as he awoke from this experience there had been a significant change for the better in his condition. There's no doubt that this experience had occurred at the crisis point of his illness. This is an account of a classic near death experience. Some people see

Spirits in or at the end of the tunnel, it would seem that if it is not your "time" then the Spirits will tell you to return. The unusual element of Barry's account is the lack of spiritual presence. I just wondered how he knew to return to the earth plane. He could not remember turning around or the journey back, just waking up to find himself in bed at home.

Just to be sure I asked Barry if he felt that he had been pre-programmed by hearing of other peoples' experiences. Barry reminded me that 40 years ago people didn't speak openly about such things, he had never heard of a similar experience.

The astral journeys made through time or over vast distances open up another area of discussion, which can be very pleasant. I know these trips can be unpleasant for some people; they can be taken backwards or forwards in time, to visit the scene of something bad. For some they are to forewarn of something unpleasant and no matter what they do, the event can't be changed, or maybe it can! This is why they are being taken and shown. Trips into the past are often used to supply answers for people who are left feeling in limbo after a negative event. A man whose wife had been killed in a car crash gave the perfect example of this to me; investigators and police couldn't provide the man with a satisfactory answer or reason for her accident. For a couple of years he imagined all kinds of scenarios, then one night he was taken on an astral journey. On this journey he observed the accident. Travelling in the car with his wife he saw exactly what had happened, what had caused the distraction that had led her to lose concentration and result in her losing control and crashing the car. A piece of grit had flown through the open window straight into her eye. She was distracted, lost control of the car resulting in the fatal crash.

My client told me that this experience had changed his life; he was then able to sleep at night and use his energy for living rather than thinking and brooding. I don't know why some of us are lucky enough to experience astral journeys like this to supply answers and some aren't. Maybe someone out there has the answer!

I always feel my own experiences of astral travel are so insignificant compared to those of other people. I once had a "trip out" which took me over beautiful countryside. As I "flew" through the air I had the sensation of wind blowing against my face. I was aware that the air temperature didn't match the weather conditions; it was winter, yet the air was pleasantly warm on my face. What I love best about astral travel is the feeling of flight and freedom that it gives you. I was able to swoop down just like a bird when I needed to take a closer look at things, there is a wonderful tickle in the stomach similar to that which you get when travelling in a car that goes over a humpback bridge a little too fast.

This particular journey that I refer to began at my home when I lived in Atherton, Lancashire. I was fascinated as I flew over the local area; I travelled on to Leigh, I recognised houses which belonged to people I knew. Then, in what felt like an instant, I was in open countryside. There were mountains and rocky hillsides. The strangest thing about astral travel for me is that I have never remembered actually deciding to return to my body. On only one occasion have I remembered entering my body. I made, what I can only describe as a "bumpy landing", it woke me up! Normally I would wake up the following morning, with my head full of memories and images from my journey.

The rocky landscape I have just described to you from my astral journey meant nothing to me at the time, I didn't recognise the place at all. A couple of years later I visited Northumberland, the moment I set eyes on the rocky hillside around Cragside near Rothbury, and the rolling countryside of Central Northumberland, it was all so familiar. I said to myself "I've been here before!"

I believe that we all make astral journeys on a regular basis. More often than not we have no recall, often those who do remember these experiences prefer to describe them as "a vivid dream"; it's much easier to deal with that way! I am beginning to wonder if there is any such thing as a normal dream!

When writing the original script of this book I had just come back from a four-day break in Cornwall and whilst there I visited the Lizard Peninsular. Exploring the coastline high above Kynance Cove, I remembered another astral journey that I had made about four years before. These two experiences were obviously predictive, but these places, Cornwall and Northumberland, are very unique. I never thought about going to discover them, yet I recognised them immediately once I had found them.

Having dealt with an example of prediction through astral travel, we move on to the subject of healing. Healing is becoming more popular as people become more open minded. Of these the laying-on of hands and absent healing are two of the best known. During my years of working as a medium and meeting thousands of people, I have only met four people who remember experiencing a healing situation whilst on an astral journey. Each time I have been given an account of such a journey, I have felt incredibly emotional and surprisingly humble.

In the earlier chapter about Lisa, we talked about Neil's dream where he visited a "spiritual hospital" in his sleep state. This was a healing experience for him. The day after the experience he was able to get on with his life not just with existing. In 1984 Ruth suffered a nervous breakdown. For two years she battled with the "monster" called depression, nothing and no one could help. People seemed to avoid or even punish her for being ill. Depression is like that; people find it a nuisance or an embarrassment. It was a very lonely and frightening time for her. She just didn't have the energy to overcome it. There was an acceptance that this is how life would be forever. Her grandfather had given her a message, through me, from the Spirit world, in a nutshell; he promised her that she would get better. Shortly after those messages were given, she was going through a particularly bad time, one night she went to bed and without sedation went to sleep. (This was a miracle to her.) That night she was taken on an astral journey, this is what happened. She found herself lying in a giant bed; the headboard was ornately carved. The bedding, she remembered, was of the highest quality, cream cotton that was very heavily embroidered with massive frills around the pillowcases. She was dressed in a silk nightgown, Victorian in style with enormous puff-sleeves and a lace ruffled yoke and collar. The most amazing thing about this situation was that she could separate her Spirit from her astral body, enabling her to move around the room and look at herself. Her skin looked clear and translucent and her hair was thick and bouncing with curls just as it had been when she was a young girl. Both her skin and hair had suffered badly during her illness, mainly due to the use of drugs; she liked what she saw.

After a few seconds, she returned to her astral body. There was a young man sitting on the bed with his back to her. He was wearing a red T-shirt and had a mop of very dark hair. At that time she didn't recognise the man as her husband, she just felt reassured and very safe.

Looking around the room Ruth noticed that there were no walls, but there was a window frame painted in a mid-green colour. She described the experience to me as "being in a cloud". The room was full of Spirits, she couldn't see them but she could sense their presence. The room was full, there were Spirits surrounding the bed, both sides and at the bottom. There was a sense of familiarity with these Spirits. The room was filled with an overwhelming feeling of love and warmth.

The following morning she awoke and felt very different. Not fully recovered from her illness, but much improved and with an in-built belief that she was on the way to recovery. The details of the astral journey were very vivid in her memory, she could recall every detail, but she had to admit that it didn't make sense at the time. She had a "knowing" that there was a profound reason for being taken on this journey. It was to receive healing, she just didn't realise it at the time. When she discussed the experience with her husband, she was suddenly aware that the man on the bed was he, but he didn't have any recollections of an astral journey the previous night.

In the next few weeks her health started to improve slowly but surely. Things, and maybe I should say life, started to make sense. When a person suffers a nervous breakdown, nothing seems to make sense or have any value attached to it. The sense of purpose in life is lost as well as the loss of motivation and drive to carry on living.

I won't describe this is a miracle cure, but it was a turning point. Even though I was very close to Ruth throughout this terrible time of her life, I was also an observer. I believe that if the Spirit world had not stepped in and helped her at that time, it is highly probable that she would not be alive today. I have no proof of that; I just speak from instinct. This is what I would describe as one of the ultimate spiritual experiences, I have heard of only one other astral journey with the purpose of healing. I know it sounds fantastic, but that is because it is. I'm sure there are many people in the world that have had a similar experience to this one but who feel too afraid to tell anyone for fear of being judged. My opinion is that the world is changing, people are becoming more open minded.

I wish to end this chapter with one of my own astral journeys. My Spirit went to meet another a spirit in a specially created place that I like to call a kind of "twilight zone" or "special place". It is a dimension created for us, as we can't enter the Spirit world fully until it is our time to do so.

Have you ever woken up in the morning and said something like "I had the most amazing dream last night, I spent time with my mother and now I feel that she is still with me" or "I can't get her out of my mind"? Over the years this has happened to me on about half a dozen occasions. I have often had dreams featuring departed family and friends, however anyone who has been lucky enough to have one of these "reunions" will know that they aren't dreams, they really are the most wonderful experiences and they stay with us forever.

I feel that I have, on one occasion, met up with my friend Jenny, my mum and dad and on two other occasions, my Dalmatian Jenny. The one I want to tell you about is when I met my father-in-law Frank Harold.

Martin and I met when I was 41 and he was 48. There was so much catching up to do, getting to know about each other's personal history and family backgrounds. This has always been important to me. Martin's dad Frank Harold passed to Spirit when he was 68 and Martin just 17 years old. I have been told so much about him, what a wonderful character he was, I was very sad that I would never get a chance to meet him; not in this life anyway! He was a pharmaceutical chemist; he was a manager for Boots the Chemist and carried on as a relief manager after his retirement.

The astral experience I had was about 3 or 4 years after Martin and I got together. During my experience I walked into a Boots store similar to the one near us in Bridgnorth, very modern, just as it is today, nothing like Boots would have been in Frank's time. I asked the assistant if I could speak to the chemist, as I wanted advice on

Frank Harold Foulser, manager, Boots the Chemist, London SW17.

photography. She asked me to wait a moment whilst she spoke to him; I did, she returned, "The chemist will be with you shortly" she said. I waited and he appeared from the back room, it was Martin's dad. We just looked at each other, said nothing, he walked around the counter, put his arms around me and gave me the most fantastic hug. He was wearing his tweed sports jacket and I was so aware of the texture of the fabric as my arms wrapped around him. The best way I can describe this hug is "all consuming", just beautiful. The next thing I remember was waking up with the feeling of his arms still tightly wrapped around me. From that moment I felt such love for him, it's never waned and I don't feel too upset that I never got to the chance to meet him in this life. I really feel that I have been introduced and I know for sure that one day I will meet him again, when I go to the Spirit world - but I'm not in a rush; I've got a lot of living to do in this world yet!!

Chapter Twenty-Four

How to use Mediumship

I would suggest that it is virtually impossible to pick a medium out in a crowd. They come in all shapes and sizes, colours and creeds. I recall the early days of my career, when I was just 30, something still makes me smile. It is the number of occasions I opened my door to be greeted by a client saying, "hello I've come to see your mother". It would seem that the most popular image of a medium in people's minds is that of an old lady dressed in black, huddled around an open file and reading tealeaves. For others, it is an old lady dressed in long flowing robes with a black cat close at hand.

I have never fitted either of these descriptions. For a while my youth and fresh new approach to mediumship caused me a few problems, clients' did not take me seriously. In time, not only did they take me seriously, but also embraced my style and fresh new approach to spiritual matters. The spiritualist church provides a training ground for some wonderful mediums who then go on to do one-to-one work, as well as working on the platform in churches. They progress through a formal training, far removed from my own spiritual/psychic development. I believe in keeping things simple, plain speaking and calling a spade a spade. (Maybe you have already realised this about me!)

I set out, years ago, to change the face of mediumship, for those who wanted it. I wanted to make it more appealing to young people. I feel that I have achieved this; I feel it's no use seeking help when the mistakes have already been made. I subscribe to he theory that prevention is better, or easier than, cure. I also felt that men had been excluded or discouraged from having settings. I wanted to open my door to all, so I did and it worked.

The majority of my clients are under 40 and many are under 30. People, including men, are becoming more emotionally needy. They also seek comfort and spiritual advice and see this as adding a new dimension to their life. If used well by the client and administered professionally and tactfully, not forgetting to mention honestly, by the medium, it's a wonderful asset to enhance anyone's life.

Each medium has an individual way of working, so it is very difficult to compare each with another. A medium that suits one person may not suit someone else. Recommendations are fine but at the end of the day, people must make up their own minds about who is "good" and who isn't.

The advice I would give to everyone who visits a medium for the first time, whether through a recommendation or an advertisement, is just go with an open mind, expecting nothing, that way everything you are given by way of information or messages from the Spirits is a bonus.

The one thing that is always guaranteed to "put me off", before I have even started the sitting, is an opening statement from the client "I've heard you are very good" or "my friends thinks you are marvellous". This is lovely to hear, extremely positive feedback but it automatically puts me on a pedestal, and expectations are very high. I always do my best for everyone, however statements like that make me feel as though my client has placed a mountain in front of me, then said "Climb that for me!" Creating tension as you can appreciate, the secret to quality mediumship is relaxation.

No matter what style of mediumship/psychic skill is used whether it be Tarot, Crystal Ball, Rune Stones or Clairvoyance, I'm sure most people will agree that the hardest detail to give is timescale. I base this fact on years of receiving feedback from clients. I've never ceased to be amazed how accurate, or inaccurate, time that has been predicted can be. When clients have spoken to me about sittings that they have had with other psychics or mediums, it is the accuracy of timescale that seems to be the one thing on which they place their judgement as to whether a medium is any good or not.

Turning the spotlight on myself as someone's client for a moment, I've just looked through a notebook, which I have kept. It has in it my notes taken during personal sittings, which I have experienced over many years. The content is quite amazing, most predictions have materialised, and some things that happened were out of my control. The others have been opportunities, some of which I took, others I dismissed or avoided; nevertheless the predictions were correct. Time does vary, some things happened bang on time, a few surprised me and happened earlier, but many things seemed to drag their heels. I recall that in the past I have thought the medium to be wrong, when an event or a new person entering my life had not materialized by the given time. Very rarely has the sitting been wrong and I have found myself apologising profoundly for doubting the Spirit's information or the medium's ability. Some events have been as long as 12 to 18 months late according to the original prediction. "Better late than never" my mum would have said.

The only explanation I can offer for this lack of accuracy involving time is the fact that time is given in "Spirit time" but time doesn't exist in the Spirit world. Time doesn't have a place, compared to the earth plane where time is a great evil; we are in general clock-watchers everyone and everything seems to be on a timer, resulting in pressure and stress. When I do my job I am expected to convert spiritual time into earth time, a very difficult task and one better not attempted. However, I do try because most people including myself feel a need to know "when?" or "how long will that take?" More advice from me is to almost take any time-scale given "with a pinch of salt", be flexible

184

when time is included in your sitting; it is the information and spiritual messages that are the most valuable ingredients.

If I were asked to divide my average sitting into percentages of prediction and advice, I would answer "25% prediction and 75% help, support and advice." The area of prediction is extremely tricky. I tell a person what I can "see" on their pathway. That is the prediction, the rest is up to them, whether they choose to take it up or avoid it is their choice. Many people believe that when something is given in a sitting then that must be the right way or choice for them. This is not always true, we are free Spirits and the choice is ours. On certain occasions a warning is attached to information, when this happens it would probably be foolish to ignore it. After all the main reason for having a sitting is for guidance.

Contrary to the thoughts and beliefs of many people, sittings are not a "cure all". They are meant to enrich our lives, enlighten us, advise and guide us. A good metaphor for a sitting is "to help a person who is wandering in the fields often in thick fog, to find his way back to the main path and, hopefully, the sign posts."

Let's talk about predictions that are "set in concrete". I know I've made many. Some I have been very pleased to make, such as financial windfalls, others have made me shudder. By "set in concrete" I mean an event that is going to happen, and nothing or no one can prevent it from doing so. Deaths are the most common of these. It's almost impossible to say to a client "you will move house" or "you will take a new job". That is the decision of that person. When I see a serious illness, which has already developed and will result in a death because it is already too advanced, then that makes a definite prediction.

I must say again that I can only speak for myself nobody else in this profession. How we use a sitting is as important as having it in the first place. I get the feeling this book is turning into the "Good Mediumship Guidebook" maybe that's not a bad thing. If, when you visit a medium, they tell you something that you don't like the sound of or that doesn't feel right, do ask "is that changeable?" Any medium worth their salt would not mind explaining things to you. Ask questions about things that trouble you, or that you did not understand. Never leave a sitting distressed or "up in the air," remember, you probably went for the sitting because you felt "up in the air". Don't expect the medium to work miracles or to heal you, although I must say that I know of a lot of healing that has taken place during sittings, this being an indirect effect rather than a direct one; a bonus if you like.

I want to tell you about Helen, a long-term client of mine. It was apparent with each sitting that her health was deteriorating due to her taking on far too many commitments and the general pressures in life were building up, a vicious circle had formed. One year when she made her regular summertime visit to me I knew instantly that this was a day for plain speaking in order to save her life. I was told that Helen had a heart problem. She had felt ill for sometime but had chosen to ignore it. Tactfully, I hope, I delivered the message from the Spirits about her heart along with the spiritual advice that if she didn't cut the workload in general down by half, she would not return to me for her next year's summer reading.

She became very tearful and said to me "so you are saying that if I don't cut back, I will die!" I replied, "Yes that is exactly what the Spirits are saying". Helen did return the following summer for her annual reading. She looked wonderful, better than I had seen her look for years. She told me that, a month after the last sitting, she had fallen ill. A heart murmur was found and angina was diagnosed. She was treated and made a recovery and was advised by the doctors to cut down her workload! She reduced her 30 hours a week to working only 15 hours and she stopped child minding her two grandchildren two days a week, which were originally her days off; her only time off!

Helen's daughter employed a child-minder and Helen enjoyed having her grandchildren for tea and for weekend outings, a pleasure instead of a chore. She also carved out for herself a social life, the first time in years. She told me her life had been all work and no play, "no wonder I was ill!" Play being the keyword here as she had just joined the amateur dramatic society. Helen told me that when I had told her in the last reading that she was ill, she hadn't wanted to hear that, so she chose to ignore it, very foolishly. When she collapsed, the words of the reading flooded into her mind, she made the decision there and then, that if she survived this trauma she would change her lifestyle because she knew what would happen if she didn't.

I really believe that if Helen had not had the reading she would have got back on her feet and carried on in her old pattern. The reading played a vital part in saving her life.

When I have a reading I must admit that I have a bad habit of sticking a label or tag onto each piece of information or person that I am told about. For example, if I'm told that there will be a death in the family, I fly to the obvious, I assume that it will be the person who is ill or the elderly frail relative. How wrong I have been on many occasions. The most distressing example for me was, when I was told a family member would die suddenly within six months. At that time there were a few people who could have been likely candidates to fulfil this prediction. But how wrong I was, my cousin Brian who was just 29 years old, collapsed and died with pulmonary oedema. I was devastated; nothing could have prepared me for that.

Mediums aren't God; they don't have the power to single out individuals and say, "it's their turn next" however, they are able to prepare us for a shock. As if to place a cushion under us to absorb the shock when the news breaks. It is best to be open-minded and prepared, as far as possible, for a passing, nothing can stop the pain but prior knowledge of such an event can aid the grieving process; if only in as much as to know that the Spirit world was preparing for their arrival, they are not lost or wandering souls, they are safe.

The information that is clear and detailed is straightforward; one should either act on the advice or store it and wait, whatever is appropriate. If things are unclear or veiled there's a reason for that, time will reveal all. Maybe it would hinder our natural progress in life if we knew too much too soon. So, if you're a person with very limited patience, or you must know every detail, please take my advice and don't have a sitting, it really isn't for you.

Going over my own experience of having sittings has highlighted just how much they are open to misinterpretation. Reading my notes, certain predictions, which have since manifested themselves, are not as expected. I can clearly recall how I interpreted the information on the day of the sitting, what I thought it would be and how things would develop, compared with what actually happened, I couldn't have been further from the truth. Take and wait is the best advice that I can give, even if it is not the easiest of policies.

Have you ever made a decision to change something in your life, if not the whole of your life? Then done it and realised that you have swapped one set of problems for another. It could have been that you thought that making a change would make everything perfect then it didn't turn out like that. This is because all things in life have a flip side, just like a coin, it's all about balance. I believe that life must have balance; all things in life have these two sides. So, when a prediction is made and it sounds wonderful to you, know that there will be an element of it that is hidden. Get into the habit of asking your medium questions e.g. "if, when this new man comes into my life, I take up his proposal of marriage, will it be successful and what are the negatives relating to this man and the situation?" I have used what I call a classic example here, because so many people are searching for love and happiness and no one is perfect. There's a tendency to believe that if a person is predicted to them then they are perfect or even superhuman because they have been spiritually announced.

Looking at the flip side of this coin, when bad news or a warning is given, there is more often than not a positive side to it, although this is hardly ever visible at the time of the sitting, for example; the man told about a member of staff embezzling money from his firm was not a happy man, but on the positive side after the situation had been addressed and the culprit removed, he could have peace of mind and be financially better off in the future.

187

Chapter Twenty-Five

My own Psychic/Spiritual Experiences

When I was a child, I didn't see any ghosts, my brother Danny seemed to be the one who was "blessed" with these experiences, although I don't think he would agree with the word blessed. Nor did I hear voices in my ear; I was never a young Doris Stokes. The strongest experiences I recall were the sensing of spiritual presence in our home, which I have already told you about earlier in the book. There were a few occasions when my eyes caught a fleeting glimpse of a dark shadow in the room. At that time I put it down to a trick of the light as many people do. Sometimes it's more comfortable to do that.

The " Poltergeist period" seemed to be the time when I noticed a heightening of my spiritual awareness. I always feel that this was a direct result of sitting with a group of girls; all of us aged about 16, in the school medical examination room having séances! These took place during "free periods", we were at the top of the school and we had a lot of time to spare. We didn't have a Ouija board; we used squares of paper instead, each with a letter or number written on and an upturned glass. There's no doubt that we would've been expelled had we been discovered, but we weren't! It was fascinating and scary. We sat around the table, about six of us. We placed our index finger very lightly on the up-turned glass. Very slowly the glass started to move, first moving to one letter, then another. (I'm tingling as I simply recall the experience and write about it for you.) We were given lots of messages which, when we enquired of family members about the content, proved to be correct. We became addicted and only stopped the sessions when the school year ended.

It sounds wonderful doesn't it? We were very lucky, nothing untoward happened to us. However, this is not as innocent as it sounds. It is not a party game. For many it has proved to be a dangerous and distressing practice. Even though I did it then, and own up to attending this type of séance on a few occasions in my adult life, one of which went very wrong. I would not do it now and I beg people not to dabble, leave this sort of thing to the professionals.

As I get older and wiser, I look back on that time in the medical examination room at school and I feel that it was my participation in these sessions that helped my "trapdoor" to open. This is how I like to describe it, when it is open, spiritual communications flow. I don't go around with it open all the time; I can close it and "switch off" if I like. That is part of the psychic development, learning to switch on and off. I must add that occasionally I sense a presence or "know" information without trying. Usually the information is quite important or useful. 12 years passed after those sessions in the school medical room before I realised that I had something "going on" in that department. The years between 16 and 28 were psychically uneventful, nothing spectacular to report apart from some dreams which were predictive, but nothing to get excited about at all. My stronger psychic and spiritual experiences occurred along with, and after, my mediumship developed. Compared to many people, I have "seen" a lot, but I have met many that are to be envied when one hears their catalogue of experiences. The sense of "knowing" and feeling spiritual presence is an on-ongoing thing, I have learned to live with it. Don't misunderstand me I'm not blasé about this; it's simply part of life now. Maybe if it stopped, I would feel a sense of loss, just as someone does if they lose a limb or one of their five senses.

My home at the moment is in Much Wenlock, Shropshire. When we moved here in June 1996 we lived in a house, which was filled with feelings of sadness and tragedy. These feelings were confirmed when a neighbour told me that the young lady who had lived next door, had passed to Spirit very tragically in the January, six months before we arrived. She was about 26 and had been pregnant; she died of toxaemia. I was relieved to know that my feelings had been correct. In the November of that year her widower and two small children moved out. I was aware of the difference, she no longer visited him here, she had moved on with him. The sad and tragic feelings moved with her.

I was then surprised to keep getting more feelings of tragedy; it started around Christmas time. I knew this also was a lady, but I couldn't get to the bottom of it so I made some gentle enquiries and discovered that the lady, who had lived in our house a few years earlier, had died very traumatically through choking on her own vomit. Her name was Margaret and I often felt her, but never saw her. In the June of 1997, my sister came to visit me and she saw her very clearly in the dining room. She described the lady to me, so I checked this out and the description was perfect right down to the clothes she was wearing. I don't know why Margaret didn't approach me, but I feel that she enjoyed living with us most of the time and she was very welcome, maybe one day I shall be able to help her. I just know she's restless about certain situations that she left behind when she passed to Spirit. We have left that house now but Margaret often comes to me when I go for a sitting and she even joined in when I went to see medium Stephen O'Brien perform a clairvoyant demonstration at a local theatre in October 2004. My Dalmatian Jenny also joined us on that occasion, it was very emotional for me and I was thrilled that they got through.

Throughout this book I have told you about experiences I have had whilst working with clients, from being touched, to being prodded and poked. Now I want to tell you just how pathetic I am when it comes to the situations when I have seen Spirits. I used to think, "I'm not brave at all", but bravery has nothing to do with it when a Spirit materialises itself in front of you. Especially when that Spirit is someone you recognise. I say this because, quite often when people see Spirits, they are strangers and somehow that isn't quite as shocking as seeing one's mother, father or friend; that is how I feel, others may feel differently.

When I have seen the Spirit of someone I know, my eyes are clearly opposing my brain. My eyes are saying "I know that person" but my brain is saying, "I can't to be seeing this person, they are now dead!" The internal conflict is tremendous. For me it's never easy to deal with, but I only speak for myself. Some people just experience it and enjoy it. I must add that I'm getting better at handling visual experiences as I get older.

I have been awakened on many occasions in the middle of the night. My eyes seem to have sprung open and an overwhelming feeling has filled me with a desire to turn my head and look towards a certain area of the room. Usually this would be the opposite side of the bed, when I did, on each occasion I would see someone standing there, looking on. I recall two such occasions both a number of years ago. On the first occasion I saw a tall dark figure of a man he had very broad shoulders. Even though it was very dark, his features became clear in my mind (clairvoyance). After some discussion the morning after, my husband confirmed that the man that I had seen was his grandfather. Shortly before this incident, we were both woken from our sleep by the sound of tapping on the wardrobe door. The noise woke me from a deep sleep, at first I thought I was dreaming, but as the sound got louder, it was evident that the noise was from inside the room. On this day neither of us would look to see who was doing the tapping. I must tell you, I decided to slip down underneath the covers and my curiosity did not get the better of me!

Afterwards I thought "what a coward I am". When the Spirit gentlemen turned up a few weeks later, I knew immediately that he had been the one tapping on the wardrobe door. The reason for his visit was to forewarn me of a personal crisis that was to follow shortly. after his visit. It is my experience that the Spirits make visits for a reason. They are either as a warning, to give comfort and support or to share a joyous time.

A second night time visitor that I wish to tell you about I call "the grey lady", it sounds corny doesn't it? When she appeared to me one night, again standing at my husband's side of the bed, she seemed to have a film or veil in front of her, yet she was very clear. She wore a paisley wrap-over pinafore apron; her hair was very neatly rolled up at the back of her head. Her arms were crossed in front of her, supporting her huge breasts. I called her "the grey lady" because she had a grey cast all over her, blotting out any colour. I stared at her, and she at me. She was serious but not stern. I was extremely surprised to see her standing there, but I was not scared, as I had been on so many other occasions. I instinctively knew who she was, Ellen, my husband's grandmother. After a short time I did turn away and tried to ignore her. As I write today, many years after the event, I feel very embarrassed about my behaviour. I'm much better these days at handling spiritual experiences in general.

I lived at my house in Atherton near Manchester for 12 years. The bedroom in that house was like a magnet for Spirits. I'm not sure if it was the room, or if it was I who attracted them, however, this is the place where I experienced most spiritual/psychic activity before I moved to Much Wenlock. A few months before my dad passed to Spirit, I was sitting reading a book one night by soft light. I felt drawn, when I looked across the room, there, as plain as day, I could see a very slim young lady. She was standing in front of the chest of drawers her back towards me, her head bowed forward, as though she was reading or looking at something. She had the most beautiful long red wavy hair and she was wearing a long cream nightdress; she looked rather like a figure from a Pre-Raphaelite painting.

Thankfully, this was yet another occasion that I managed not to scream or jump up and run because the feelings that she brought were of calmness and tranquillity. She moved slightly, I caught a glimpse of the side of her face and she was very beautiful. I just looked at her for a few moments, (it's always difficult to be precise about time when describing spiritual experiences) and then she just dissolved into thin air. This is probably the most pleasant spiritual experience I have had. To this day I can't explain her visit, who she was and why she came, but she was very welcome.

It has come to my notice that the Spirits do like electricity! Many of my clients have told me of their experiences where electricity has been involved. I have a number of my own tales to tell. In 1996 I met a physicist, Andrew Green, who specialised in paranormal activity. He had done research into ghosts and found Spirits can alter or affect anything that functions with infrared or radio waves such as TV and video. In the last few years I have had a number of experiences of this kind, the most prominent ones involved my stereo and, especially, the tape recorder section of it. The periods leading up to the passing of my sister in law Irene in 1991 and my sister Freda in 1994 were very active in this department. The Spirits would activate the record button as I was listening to a tape. I have one particular tape with blank spots dotted through it. Before Freda passed over, they often activated the tape either to record or simply to play music, I instantly knew something was very wrong. Sadly she passed over on the 1st January 1994 just a few days after I last visited her in hospital.

The house in Much Wenlock, where we lived when we first moved to Shropshire, has been a hive of psychic activity where electrical interventions are concerned. Not just the stereo but also the TV. There they enjoyed turning the radio on in the middle of the night.

The odd thing is the noise only ever woke one of us up. If it was Martin who woke first, it was usually an indicator that there was, or would be, a problem surrounding him, if it happened to me, then it would relate to me in some way. It has proved to be very accurate as an early warning system!

The television was the same early warning system, we could be sitting relaxing, then suddenly the sound would blast out making us jump out of our skins, or the volume would be turned down. Sometimes the colour would be turned off or the picture would become so bright that it hurt our eyes. On some occasions they would treat us to a combination of excess colour and sound!! It would seem that the amount of disruption related to the nature or intensity of the problem coming up. We moved to a new home in 1999, a converted pub, I could write a separate book about the "goings on" here; one day I probably shall!

I don't think for one moment that any of this is unique. I know for a fact that this sort of activity takes place every day all over the world; it's just that I've decided to talk about it. Others have done in books, articles and TV programs; however, we are only a small number compared to the amount of spiritual and psychic activity that is happening out there. I just feel it's time for us to talk and be more open, to become more open minded and accepting of such things, rather than dismissing these experiences, sweeping them under the carpet.

I know that a lot of what I have included in this chapter isn't exceptional, especially when compared to the experiences of others, but they are to me because they are my experiences. In 1990 I had what must be my most amazing and intense experience, it took place on Christmas Eve. I went to bed at 11.30 feeling very tied, I must have gone to sleep literally as soon as my head touched the pillow. Then at exactly 12.25, according to my digital clock, my eyes opened. I lay still for a moment, looking at the figures on the clock. My first thoughts were "goodness it's dark in here". Then I became aware of a strange atmosphere, impossible to describe apart from perfect stillness yet with an element of tension in the air. I felt my eyes being drawn to the bottom of the bed, slowly as I looked across the room, I could seek two figures, two women holding hands. They seemed to be cocooned in a bubble, the whole image was grey in colour but appeared luminous, and there was no difficulty in seeing them even though the night was so black.

They were very clear and solid, yet only visible from the waist up. They looked across towards me with such stone-faced expressions which I would like to describe as, "if looks could kill" expressions. At first I was shocked and stunned at their appearance, then, in what must have been seconds but felt like hours, I just screamed out, then dived under the covers. I had waited for almost five years to see the Spirit of my mum, she had visited my younger sister on a few occasions and I must admit I felt left out. Not only was I graced with a visit from her that Christmas Eve, but there was a bonus, she brought with her my auntie Ada, mum's sister who had only recently passed over to Spirit in the November of that year. I say brought with her because there was something in the way that mum was clasping Ada's hand that suggested mum had led the way.

This was not a pleasant experience; it was a warning for me. The year that lay ahead was difficult and sad, in the March I was quite ill, and this really set me back. In the July my Dalmatian Jenny died, followed by the sad loss of my sister in law Irene in the September. These were the major upsets, but there were also many more minor ones.

When I awoke on Christmas morning I felt "hung over". The experience stunned me just like a heavy drinking session and the memory of it had the same effect as a hangover. It was in the hours that followed that I realised that I must prepare myself for a bad time.

I haven't seen my mum since that night; however, she is around me so much. She usually makes her presence felt by bringing the beautiful fragrance of freesias, her favourite flowers. This takes place in the house, car or outside and often in winter when there isn't a flower in bloom, if there were, this may offer a logical explanation for the fragrance. I much prefer this gentle form of communication; it suits my personality. After her visit, I said to my friend Jim Walker, "if this is how she wants to visit me I would rather she did not bother! "

I realise, as I write, that I could go on and on giving you accounts of my experiences. But I won't, I will work on the theory that a taste of something can be nicer than a belly full. I still have the opinion that other people's experiences are more interesting or exciting than mine are, but I will let you be the judge of that!

If any readers have had any kind of Spiritual or psychic experience that they would like to share with others, probably in a future book, as I hope to write more, please don't hesitate to contact me either direct if you have my contact details, or through my publishers. I'm waiting to hear from you.

Chapter Twenty-Six

Where do I go from here?

I began the first draft of this book in April 1996 whilst living in East Sussex and I'm writing the final draft in June 2005 in Shropshire. It feels to me as if I have completed a journey or journeys, one into the past, another into the deep corners of my mind and heart. I certainly had to brush aside "dust and cobwebs" to resurrect some memories. There is also the physical journey that the pile of notebooks and papers has made.

I can honestly say, as I look back on my life, that it has never been easy for one reason or another. I know lots of people can say this but I can only speak for myself. I made the decision, at the end of 1994, that "enough was enough" and to get out and "spread my wings". During the following 12 months I finished the psychology training that I was doing and qualified, I met Martin, now my husband, I stopped doing "face to face" readings. 12 years is long enough doing the same thing. I escaped from my old life and it felt like "jumping off a cliff". I landed, but not on my feet! I have, with Martin at my side, been "finding my feet" but it has taken 10 years. I hope this inspires any reader who also feels that "enough is enough", to take a leap out into the unknown.

It is my belief that things never stay the same in life, just like the changing seasons. There's a constant pattern of birth, death and even re-birth. We, as people, are constantly changing. Sometimes it is very difficult to see, from our standpoint, exactly where we're heading in life or in the future, "not being able to see the wood for the trees". I've realised the value of two sayings, the first being "in order to know where you're going in the future, it is important to know where you came from". Also "familiarity breeds contempt" yes, familiarity is safe, easy and comfortable. If we make changes or change ourselves, it doesn't always meet with the approval of people around us because they have to think about us in a different way – the loss of familiarity can mean the loss of control or quite simply for many, that can be much too hard work!

Having noticed that if we stay doing the same things or following the same old routines for too long, something happens to "rock our boat". This could be a close death, a health problem, redundancy or many other things, even a lottery win. Not all changes are created because of negative events or situations. I have realized that if we won't change things, then life throws something at us, which often leaves us with no choice, the changes are made for us.

When I left my second marriage in 1995, I had no idea just how much disruption and change would be created by my actions. Probably it was better not to know, or maybe I wouldn't have stepped forward into the unknown. For many of us, we have had to wade through so much mud in order to get to the "green fields". For me, I am standing on the edge of the "green fields" and things are getting easier but there have been times when I thought I would never get a glimpse of the fields, never mind reach them. This is called risk; I was brought up in a "no risk" zone. Now I'm a higher-risk, adventurous person and intend to carry on being so.

Since 1995 I have found periods of "free time" which I have taken advantage of and written this book. Initially to get it all down on paper, then at a later date to re-write it. Following a gap of a few years I have altered it, brought it up-to-date and approached my publisher. If I am honest the latter was done not just because of "free time" but because the time now feels right.

Since 1983 I have done one sort of spiritual work or another, I feel time for a change yet again. What I do know is that I always want to be involved in spiritualism. I want to find or develop other ways of using it, this book being one of them. I realise that having a sitting is, for so many people, a "life saver" or as one man told me "a breath of fresh air". Part of me feels guilt when I say, "I don't want to do one-to-one work forever", however, there's a bigger part of me that is filled with exciting ideas, to work with and help people. There will always be good mediums that can give sittings. One thing that I have never felt is indispensable; people will always be able to find another psychic or a medium. I believe that most things in life have a psychic or spiritual aspect to it, so I feel the world is my oyster, it's up to me to make careful choices.

I was lucky enough to meet David Pinnegar in 1995, a physicist who owns Hammerwood Park in East Sussex. This he told me, after taking part in a "Spookathon" in his historic house, "I'm a scientist, but after this I have to say that I believe". Before I met my husband, Martin, he lived in a very "spiritually sterile environment", what a shock to his system when he met me, with my background! Well they do say that opposites attract, and with us that has certainly been true. I'm glad to say he is now much more open-minded. He plans to do some psychic research of his own in the future. He's very positive about it; he too has a scientific background and believes there is so much to know from a positive approach, proving that there are Spirits, (for those who must have tangible proof) as opposed to the common approach of proving that there are not! There's also the area of UFO's and whether there is anything psychic or spiritual connected to this phenomenon. I have to admit this concept does "blow my mind" a little, but I have already said I've become an adventurous person so maybe I shall take a look into this area with him.

My two main areas of interest are healing (and self-healing) and teaching people to use their own psychic and spiritual abilities. This does not mean training people to become mediums. Since 1995 I have tried to become more self reliant in every way. No longer living next door to my family and old friends, I've had to use my own resources. I haven't had people to rely on physically at the drop of a hat, at least not until more recently and new friends have entered my life. I was a person who liked to seek advice, answers or support. Now I've had to turn to myself for these and incredibly I've found them. I have a very reliable and supportive husband, but I feel the need to support myself more than I have done in the past. This is what I would like to do for others, to teach them to do the same and to be able to tap into their own resources. We hope to run a variety of personal development and Spiritual/ Psychic interest workshops around country in the not too distant future.

When I was 38, instinct told me that, in general, things would change, especially my work. Even though I knew it was a long way into the future, I wanted to prepare. With good advice and strong support, I secured myself a place at Manchester University to study counselling skills. I followed that by studying Neuro Linguistic Programming for two years. First becoming a Practitioner, then a Master Practitioner. Neuro Linguistic Programming, or NLP, is the study of subjective experience and advanced communication skills. The reason I chose to study this area of psychology was because of my spiritual knowledge. It appeared to be the only area of psychotherapy that allows the client to work at a spiritual level. This is very important to me; my two areas of interest marry beautifully. I thought it was magic when I found NLP, it did not conflict with my beliefs so I don't have to change my identity when I work with a client and neither do they; it's called being true to oneself. I find the whole prospect of this kind of personal development work very exciting, just as I did when I started my career as a medium.

Things do change in life and I have learned that it is much easier to "go with the flow" than to fight it. The past is a valuable resource of learning and experience; learning to let go of the old and take hold of the new, is a wonderful skill to learn. It means you have the ability to grow and progress, I know it works because I am the living proof.

I came across this quote whilst I was thumbing through a book one day, it sort of jumped off the page and hit me between the eyes "Look to the future, as there are no regrets in that direction." This is very true, I would like to leave you with another quote this time from my friend Jenny Jones, she chanted it at me often when I consulted her regarding making decisions - "You are only passing through this way once". Please remember, "Life is for living". – Enjoy the journey!

Ann, giving an after-dinner talk to the Rotary Club in Leigh about her work
and experiences.

ISBN 1-41205520-2